Buffalo's Finest Chefs and Ingredients

By Christa Glennie Seychew

BUFFALO
· HERITAGE ·
UNLIMITED

Nickel City Chef is a Feed Your Soul production | NickelCityChef.com

Photography by Christa Glennie Seychew and, as credited:
Philipa Croft, Joseph DiDomizio, kc kratt, LEI Photography, Anna L. Miller,
Tess Moran, Nancy J. Parisi, Nate Peracciny and Matthew Quinn.

ISBN: 978-0-9825745-8-4

BUFFALO
HERITAGE
UNLIMITED

Published by Buffalo Heritage Unlimited, Buffalo, New York | BuffaloHeritage.com
Nickel City Chef: Food for Change directed by Nathan Peracciny, Buffalo, New York | Peracciny.com
Design by JCharlier Communication Design, Buffalo, New York | JCharlier.com
Printed by Zenger Boncraft, Orchard Park, New York | Zenger.com

Printed in U.S.A.

Contents

Recipes by Category

Acknowledgements

Too many cooks do not spoil the soup. The savory success of Nickel City Chef would not have been possible without the aid, support, and enthusiasm of many. I am deeply grateful to every single one of you.

First and foremost, toque off to the Nickel City Chefs: JJ Richert, who signed onto the project without hesitation and meets each challenge with a level of passion and vigor that is contagious. Krista Van Wagner, whose skill, genuine heart, and professionalism make working with her such a pleasure. Adam Goetz, whose food consistently blows away the judges and who can be counted on to do anything and everything with dedication and a smile. Brian Mietus, who is always composed, very talented and, unlike many chefs, never too busy to be polite. Paul Jenkins, whose big personality and flourish have garnered him a feverish local fan following. These chefs have dedicated their reputation, talent, and guidance to this series in ways that could not possibly be duplicated.

Without the trust and talent of the Challenging Chefs, sous chefs, judges, sponsors, farmers, and artisan food producers, I would have had neither the desire nor the ability to develop Nickel City Chef, or the book that follows the close of our third season. Hosts Bert Gambini and Mike Andrzejewski impart professionalism, levelheadedness, and grace at each and every competition. As far as I can tell, they are peerless in Western New York, and I consider myself very fortunate to have the opportunity to work with them.

Kevin Telaak, Jeff Rexinger, and the entire Artisan Kitchens & Baths crew provide us with the ultimate canvas for Nickel City Chef and manage without fail to resolve, with kindness and efficiency, the issues inherent in any live production.

Our many volunteers and staff, especially Courtney Bajdas and Michael Franco, are adept, trustworthy, and hardworking. Their loyalty to the show, the chefs, the farmers, and Feed Your Soul is inexhaustible.

Without the assistance and keen sensibilities of Rachel Fix Dominguez and the efforts of Courtney Bajdas, Lauren Newkirk Maynard, and Michael Franco, each of whom profiled some of the local sources of the secret ingredients featured in the challenges, this book might never have come to fruition. It is more beautiful than I dared imagine thanks to Christopher Schobert and Ramona Whitaker who enhanced the text with their editing ability, and Jim Charlier, whose notable design talents are evident to anyone holding this book in their hands.

A special note of appreciation goes to those who have used their skills to capture the sweaty brows and flying knives of Nickel City Chef throughout all three seasons: LEI Photography, kc kratt, Nancy J. Parisi, Nate Peracciny, Matthew Quinn, Anna L. Miller, and Joseph DiDomizio.

With much gratitude, I must acknowledge Marti Gorman, the publisher, who believed this series was destined to become a book before I did.

It is important to note here, if nowhere else, that I would not be who I am today had these people not believed in me, whether for a moment or a lifetime: Carol Harris, Kevin Telaak, Elizabeth Licata, Jennifer Goetz, Sandy Starks, Jeffrey Seychew, David Setzer, Barry Heneghan, Newell Nussbaumer, and Charlie Quill.

Finally, with gratitude and adoration, I dedicate this book to my girls, India and Sabine, who have supported my efforts tirelessly and have made every moment, no matter how challenging, worthwhile.

Christa Glennie Seychew

Foreword

BY REGINA SCHRAMBLING

Regina Schrambling is a successful nationally recognized food writer who often visits Buffalo.

After every trip here, I come home to Manhattan more convinced that Buffalo is the most overlooked food destination in New York State. But I hesitated when Christa Glennie Seychew asked me to be a judge for Nickel City Chef. Too many chef competitions are bogus, more sensational than cerebral, more P.T. Barnum than Ferran Adria. And what if the food failed? I'm notorious for being brutally honest–I knew couldn't lie.

> *"Nickel City Chef is less about glorifying individual chefs than about shining a spotlight on what really matters: local food."*

But Christa is a very persuasive person, as everyone involved in this project can attest. And I realized that Nickel City Chef is less about glorifying individual chefs than about shining a spotlight on what really matters: local food. The cook-offs and the book can only accelerate the artisanal movement here, and that's the rising tide that will lift many boats. Showcasing ingredients builds demand, which creates inspiration for other artisans and entrepreneurs and restaurateurs. Food is the future. The big industries that built the city will never come back, but the opportunities presented by cheese, meat, dairy, bread, fruits and vegetables, beer, and anything else you can eat or drink are boundless.

I've been coming to Buffalo for more than twenty-five years to visit my in-law equivalents, and the food has never let this professional eater down. I don't eat chicken, so the wing cliché never gained much traction with me, and I've decided beef on 'weck is not worth the one-note letdown unless Mike Andrzejewski turns it into sushi. My impressions are more of real food, and it just gets better and better. What makes this a singular city is the dominance of independents–the chains that have homogenized American cuisine in the rest of the country have not managed to engulf and devour Buffalo.

Even when menus are predictably in the Sinatra vein, the cooking is heartfelt. Mom-and-pop restaurants that care really care, and diners who want familiarity and plenty of it, enough to doggy-bag home, are well-served. But the most innovative chefs are the ones who are going to take Buffalo further, and Nickel City Chef is making it easier for them to get recognition in a world connected by the Internet. My consort's father was always very good at keeping up with places for us all to try, but he relied on the newspaper. After he went off to that four-star restaurant in the sky, we started taking the suggestions of readers who wrote to me on my website; now diners anywhere can see what the best chefs can do, and social media can spread those videos even farther.

> *"People travel to eat, and in Buffalo they get the bonus of art museums and architecture; these types of tourists tend to have more adventurous tastes, not to mention deeper pockets."*

I hate the pompous word culinary, but attach it to "tourism" and you can visualize even more potential for ripple effects from Nickel City Chef. People travel

Foreword

> *"I had tasted some dishes that would be at home in Manhattan or Paris. The chefs' cleverness was rivaled only by the depth of understanding of what they were working with."*

to eat, and in Buffalo they get the bonus of art museums and architecture; these types of tourists tend to have more adventurous tastes, not to mention deeper pockets (or higher lines of credit). Nickel City Chef awareness could also draw out-of-towners to neighborhoods being transformed into urban farms, one of the best trends anywhere. The industrialization of agriculture has removed Americans from the food supply; here it's up close and personal.

In the meantime, Nickel City Chef is pushing chefs to aim higher. Certainly I never expected to encounter what I did last spring, when Painted Meadows duck eggs were the secret ingredient. I went in agonizing about grading on the curve and finished thinking I had tasted some dishes that would be at home in Manhattan or Paris. The chefs' cleverness was rivaled only by the depth of understanding of what they were working with. Bonus: all those who came to the competition could buy those duck eggs from the farmer herself and taste them for themselves.

And that's an illustration of how Nickel City Chef is a bridge between the professional and the amateur. Food in this country now improves from the top down–chefs take risks and inspire home cooks. The recipes collected from the first seasons all send the same message: *do* try this at home.

The fact that we could go to the Elmwood-Bidwell Farmers' Market on our last trip and in one stop forage restaurant-quality everything for dinner–grass-fed beef, a local variety of potatoes, great tomatoes, squash and corn, fresh basil, plus Niagara wine–is just the latest validation of the food scene in Buffalo.

For many years I've been telling people: If you have to go to Buffalo, you will eat very well. These days I urge people to go voluntarily. And Nickel City Chef makes the case for me.

Regina Schrambling is a food writer and cookbook author best known as snarkmistress of her acerbic website, Gastropoda.com, which skewers absurdities in the food world (and shares her gastronomic travel experiences). When not obsessively Tweeting, she contributes to *Plate, Slate, Culture, Edible Manhattan, Gourmet Live* and *Endless Vacation* and blogs at Epicurious.com. Her resumé includes chef training at the New York Restaurant School, and stints as deputy editor of the *New York Times* Dining section and contract writer for the *Los Angeles Times* Food section. Anthony Bourdain has called her "the angriest person writing about food." Regina lives in Manhattan with her consort of nearly 30 years, Buffalo native Bob Sacha, an award-winning multimedia producer, and their famously omnivorous Siamese, Wyl-E.

Nickel City Chef: The Story

N utrient-rich soil, access to one of the world's largest sources of fresh water, and a dizzying array of microclimates are just some of the geographic features that set Western New York apart agriculturally. This part of New York state, bordered by Lake Erie to the west and Canada to the north, has exceptional conditions for growing a nearly endless variety of produce and raising livestock of all kinds, including some of the country's finest dairy cattle. Also to be found are stone fruit, wine grapes, and maple syrup.

Agriculture is a major economic driver in New York State and particularly important to the Western New York region. Wyoming County contributes the largest volume of milk to the state's dairy industry. Chautauqua County has more farms than any other county statewide. Erie County, home to Buffalo, New York's second largest city, is flush with urban farms, artisan food makers, and farmers' markets. Notably, many of the more than 7,500 Western New York farms are family-owned and -operated.

The independent spirit so typical of farmers is shared by local chefs, many of whom dream of opening their own restaurant where they can realize their creative vision. The exceptionally reasonable real estate prices in Western New York make their dreams more likely to happen. This is especially true of Buffalo, where, unlike other mid-size cities, there are relatively few chain restaurants, so independent establishments abound.

This glorious bounty has provided me, as a food editor, with endless material for articles. The tireless enthusiasm for cooking and ingredients I have encountered in interviews with chefs and farmers alike has been contagious, invigorating, and has made my job a very rewarding one.

In early 2008, as I thought about new ways I could continue my commitment to educating Western New Yorkers about food and bolstering the restaurants, farms, and artisan food-makers that were striving to bring Buffalo renown for more than just chicken wings, I launched Feed Your Soul, with the support of my good friend Sandra Starks. I hoped this business would allow me to connect local chefs to area farms, food fanatics to innovative restaurants, and perhaps even Buffalo to the national culinary scene. Although the Queen City is certainly revered in pub food circles for its contribution of chicken wings and beef on 'weck, the food scene I know and love offers so much more.

So I began to assemble food events that would further my

Anna L. Miller

Challenger Mary Ann Giordano presents her dishes to a panel of culinary experts in Challenge 14: Tomatoes from H2Gro.

efforts to enlighten and educate. First on my itinerary was a bus trip designed for chefs to the Chautauqua Institution in the southwest corner of New York State to hear author Michael Ruhlman and farm-to-table chef Dan Barber speak. The tour sold out, and it presented an excellent opportunity for the chefs and a handful of foodies to meet and get to know one another while discussing the political food issues of the day.

A few weeks later I coordinated our first annual Foodie-to-Farm tour, one of the most important events I would ever assemble. At the time, very few Western New York chefs were sourcing local food. So I invited thirty of them to join us on a bus tour that visited four local farms. The weather was glorious and, as the chefs and restaurant owners walked the fields beside the farmers who owned them, tasting sun-warmed tomatoes and peppers as they strolled, relationships were forged. Today, nearly two dozen Western New York restaurants go out of their way to incorporate local food items into their menus all year long, while dozens more source local produce during the height of the growing season. While Feed Your Soul cannot take sole credit for fueling that new direction, our efforts have had a lasting and measurable impact.

While I was encouraged by how quickly these events sold out, I found I was still not entirely satisfied. As a food editor and a community-minded individual, I wanted Buffalo to be seen by outsiders for more than just lost football games, greasy food, and snow. But I was also keenly aware of how often I found myself in conversations with local residents, trying to convince them that there are skilled chefs in their neighborhood restaurants who prepare noteworthy dishes. More often than not, the local resident would extol the huge, cheap portions they associate with their hometown, and disagree that notable cuisine and world-class dining experiences are available in Buffalo.

Worse yet, many of the chefs I had come to know claimed

they couldn't sell game meats or fresh fish to their customers. They bemoaned the fact that when unique or exotic items were offered on their specials menus, their regular customers balked. Certainly this wasn't the case in every restaurant, and some upscale establishments enjoyed greater latitude, but our best white-tablecloth restaurants are places that typical Western New Yorkers may visit only on special occasions. While my initial goal had been to improve the national perception of Buffalo's dining scene, I realized I had just as much to prove to my fellow Western New Yorkers.

Then I met Kevin Telaak, vice president of Artisan Kitchens & Baths, a high-end appliance retailer located in a turn-of-the-century stove warehouse. I had heard that his showroom kitchens were worth visiting, so I called and made an appointment. I had no idea that nestled away in the Black Rock neighborhood of Buffalo, just blocks from my home, was a breathtaking, fully refurbished demonstration kitchen space. In the second floor showroom, which had been designed to allow customers to try out top-of-the-line appliances before buying them, I was delighted to find two side-by-side working kitchens faced by empty space bracketed by hand-hewn beams and exposed brick. There was more than enough room for an audience, I thought. Certainly, a culinary competition with a live audience was in order. Kevin agreed, and I returned a week later with JJ and Kevin Richert, chefs and brothers, who had just opened Torches restaurant.

Videographer Nate Peracciny captures the culinary action, delivering brilliant imagery to the audience via flat panel monitors mounted overhead.

Both were young and enthusiastic. JJ, the eldest, has energy to burn and a competitive nature. The flare for showmanship he displays tableside in the dining room of his restaurant—torching crème brulée, whipping zabaglione, pouring whiskey—told me he wouldn't shy away from the opportunity to cook in front of a large audience. He was as enamored of the Artisan Kitchens & Baths space as I was, and over the next few weeks he allowed me to pepper him with questions about equipment needs and possible rules until I had a plan for the event firmly in mind. What better way to show Buffalo its culinary talent than through live competitions which the public could witness first hand?

A team of area chefs was required, and there were quite a few from among whom to choose. I was particularly interested in working with chefs who had a long-term stake in their restaurants, either as owners or as managing partners. Not only would they reap the most benefit from the exposure and ongoing marketing efforts associated with a public competition, but they were less likely to change jobs, saving me from having to alter promotional materials and gain permission and cooperation from a new owner. I also knew that I wanted a team made up of a couple of young hotshots with a reputation to build, paired with some established chefs who could give the event standing within the restaurant community. As an avid cooking-show viewer, I also knew it was important that participating chefs have different styles and personalities, that they be accessible and identifiable to the audience, and that they enjoy a challenge.

The second chef to join the team was Adam Goetz of Sample, a highly technical chef who thrives under pressure. Chef Paul Jenkins of Tempo was a restaurant lifer and a chef others looked up to. He had worked in many of Buffalo's best kitchens and was running one of Buffalo's hottest restaurants. Both of these chefs were ideal additions, but one more chef was needed to complete our team of four Nickel City Chefs.

I invited Mike Andrzejewski, easily Buffalo's most recognizable chef. After careful consideration, he felt that he might struggle with the size of the kitchens because he was still in rehabilitation and undergoing refittings for a prosthetic leg he requires following a serious motorcycle accident. Moving quickly around Artisan's expansive kitchens simply wasn't an option for him. However, he did agree to cohost the show, and he has done a fabulous job of educating audiences throughout each competition.

When I asked Mike to recommend another talented chef with a solid culinary background to fill the final Nickel City Chef position, he suggested Krista Van Wagner of Curly's. I had never met Krista, although I knew a lot about her and was a fan of her signature line of sauces. It was evident after our first conversation that Chef Van Wagner is much like JJ Richert: born to be in the public eye and to entertain a crowd.

Bert Gambini of WBFO and I first met when he donated his well-honed master of ceremonies services at a charity dinner I chaired. We didn't have much opportunity to talk that night, but he was professional, affable, and his velvet-toned voice made all the ladies at the dinner swoon. He seemed a perfect choice to cohost the show. A lover of food and a passionate home cook, he quickly said yes, and we moved forward to begin the series in June 2009.

Nickel City Chef: The Story

I had chosen the name Nickel City Chef to identify the elite group of handpicked chefs who would be featured on each show and represent Buffalo and Western New York. A challenger would be selected from a pool of local chefs who had submitted applications. Both competitors would have one hour to prepare three courses, featuring a secret, locally sourced ingredient, and present their dishes to a panel of judges. An audience of nearly two hundred would look on, and we would hold the event, and ourselves, to the highest culinary standards.

In addition to the secret local ingredient, all of the competing chefs would have access to a Wegmans-supplied pantry of more than two hundred ingredients and would be allowed to bring twenty items, which we called "custom ingredients," from their own kitchen. These are ingredients that cannot be made within the one-hour time frame and typically reflect the unique culinary style of each chef. Krista Van Wagner's bottled hot sauce is a perfect example, as is cooking stock; items pickled, preserved, or otherwise cured in-house; confits; or bread. While not allowing the use of these items may have made the competition harder, we felt that doing so would keep the food from accurately reflecting the personality of each chef and their signature flavor profile. We have never regretted this decision.

Challenging sous chef Daniel Lawrence attends to several sauté pans on one of Artisan Kitchen & Bath's state-of-the-art stoves.

In May 2009, we put out a call for challengers. Eager chefs submitted applications, and the season was announced. *The Buffalo News* ran a story on the front page of its "City" section, and tickets for the first four shows, scheduled to take place each month from June through September, sold out in just days. Thanks to sponsor Artisan Kitchens & Baths, a staff of dedicated volunteers, and the chefs and farmers, the series was a hit. As soon as the first season wrapped up in September with "Challenge: Potatoes," we began to plan for a second series of challenges.

After having worked in the showroom through the months of July and August, we knew that our audience would be more comfortable if we moved the show to the winter months, when the cooler weather would make it easier to control the temperature indoors. A wiser, more patient woman would have waited for the winter of 2011, rather than pushing to develop an entire season of shows in the three months before January 2010, but that is not me.

That January, we announced an eight-show season. Nearly all of the shows sold out immediately, and during this season we worked on various ways to improve the audience experience. Ten flat-panel monitors were hung above the show kitchens. In addition to providing better still images of the chefs' plates during judging, it also encouraged our video staff, led by director Nate Peracciny, to use roving cameras in the kitchen during the competitions. This delivered an up-close-and-personal view of full-color, action-packed imagery to virtually every member of the audience. We also improved the sound system and began to play a slideshow of pictures from the featured farm during the introduction to each show.

Season three was a success, as well. The four-show season, which began in the winter of 2011, sold out in forty-eight hours. Chef Paul Jenkins had retired from the series, but eager to take his place was Chef Brian Mietus of Bacchus, who blended in perfectly with the existing team. We were thrilled to host Regina Schrambling, a notable former restaurant critic and talented New York City-based food writer, as a judge. Additional sponsors became involved, and the fact that season tickets sold out quickly proved that we had fans who would return to the show time and again.

Over the course of the three seasons, the Buffalo dining scene was rapidly evolving. An influx of talented chefs were opening their own restaurants, and a national spotlight focused increasingly on the importance of eating locally sourced ingredients and supporting local businesses. The country's hunger for food entertainment was growing exponentially, rapidly spreading new trends and culinary knowledge through middle America.

These trends, along with Nickel City Chefs' high standards and constant efforts to improve and refine the show, have made it successful. Many other cooking competitions are held throughout the United States and on television but, to the best of our knowledge, no other cooking competition in the country is an ongoing series open to the general public, featuring a large, live audience and a local ingredient at its core. Unlike a typical television show, at a Nickel City Chef challenge, there are no retakes or cuts.

At the end of the second season, a television producer from Minneapolis called wanting to produce something similar in that region, and we receive similar requests from across the country every month. Chefs, restaurant owners, food activists, and event planners want to know how Nickel City Chef works, what makes it successful, and how they can duplicate our efforts in their communities. Several production companies that work with major cable networks have asked to film the series. Still, no offer or opportunity has made sense for Nickel City Chef.

It is impossible to produce a show of the caliber of Nickel City Chef without genuinely talented chefs and very high quality ingredients. I firmly believe that a project cannot attract sponsors and an audience without the foundation and credibility provided by both of these. A custom facility with room for a large audience and stellar equipment is also critical, but not easy to locate in many communities. Finally, removing "Buffalo" from Nickel City Chef, something we've been asked to do more than once, is a compromise we are simply unwilling to make.

As the series has continued, more and more requests for recipes have been received from those who have attended or watched them on the Nickel City Chef website. These constant requests, along with our videographer Nate Percciny's unique ability to visually capture the essence of a person, place, or event, led us to believe that the Nickel City Chef mission could also be accomplished by telling this story. So we set about choosing the tastiest and most requested of the recipes, keeping in mind the equipment, energy, and resources available to the average cook at home.

When the chefs were asked to provide their recipes, they were also asked to modify them, using measures instead of weights and substitutions for industrial equipment–such as thermocirculators, pressure cookers, and liquid nitrogen–that most home cooks would not have. They were also encouraged to add marination or brining to their recipe if they felt it would improve the flavor, even though they didn't have time to use these techniques during the competition.

The goal is to provide readers with restaurant-quality recipes, so that the flavors and presentation displayed at each show can be achieved at home. However, our chefs cook in teams and are professionals who think nothing of

tasks that might overwhelm the average cook. It is therefore important to read through each recipe before starting to cook; some may require practice.

The DVD includes *Nickel City Chef: Food for Change*, a 46-minute documentary directed by Nate Peracciny, designed to showcase local chefs and local ingredients, and promote the farm-to-fork movement in Western New York. Also on the DVD is footage of five of the Nickel City Chef Challenges. Watching this DVD will make your mouth water and your heart sing.

In addition to Nickel City Chef, Feed Your Soul continues to present tours and events that focus on Buffalo's culinary talent and agricultural gifts. Through the ongoing support of organizations such as Wegmans, CUTCO, Taste of Buffalo, Artisan Kitchens & Baths, and *Buffalo Spree* magazine, we are able to continue to offer exclusive and unique events that showcase our region's local flavor.

Sold out audiences of nearly two hundred fill the turn-of-the-century loft showroom at each Nickel City Chef competition.

If you have not attended a Nickel City Chef competition, it is our hope that this book and DVD will show you the Western New York that we foodies have come to know and love. We want it to make you hungry for something more, because you can experience our edible beauty yourself quite easily. Visit a local farmers' market, or search online for farm tours and genuine agricultural experiences available in your area. Eat at locally owned, independent restaurants. After a few visits you'll get to be a regular, and find a truly satisfying experience that is nearly impossible to obtain in the realm of chain restaurants. Try something new or, better yet, cook something new. Dig up your grandmother's recipes. Preserve fruit for winter. Find a butcher or baker who can answer questions about their hard-earned skills, or try buying produce you don't recognize from a roadside stand in the country. Read and support publications that feature reviews and recipes from local restaurants. Start a food blog.

Be inspired by *Nickel City Chef*–this book that chronicles the series to-date, its chefs, and its farmers. Food is a unifying common denominator among humans, so take hold of it, embrace it, and make it an important–and exciting–part of your life.

The Cast

The expertise and enthusiasm of a broad array of individuals, from camera operators to graphic designers, sous chefs to restaurant owners, farm hands to event volunteers and attendees, have propelled Nickel City Chef from mere concept to a successful event. Prime among this large cast of hardworking and dedicated Western New Yorkers are the Nickel City Chefs, the hosts, the judges, and some key people within important organizations who believed in the idea and found creative ways to support it.

THE CHEFS

Nickel City Chef Adam Goetz of Sample
Seasons 1-3

Buffalo native Adam Goetz spent his youth in the kitchen, where he learned to love cooking. As an adult he worked in several local restaurants before moving to Colorado, where he served as executive sous chef at the revered Castle Pines Country Club. Next, Goetz returned to the East Coast, taking a job as executive chef saucier at the famed Waldorf Astoria Hotel in New York City. It was there that he adopted the Waldorf's mantra: "The difficult immediately, the impossible may take a couple of minutes."

While at the Waldorf, Goetz's responsibilities included updating the classic Bull & Bear Steakhouse and modernizing the hotel's bistro, Oscar's Restaurant. After a few years Goetz was asked by the owners of Buffalo's Park Lane Restaurant to shepherd the reopening of their catering facilities at the Statler Towers and serve as the distinguished eatery's executive chef. He jumped at the opportunity to return to Buffalo, where he started a family with his muse, wife, and business partner, Jennifer.

Eventually the couple decided to open their own restaurant, Sample, a concept-driven eatery on the west end of Buffalo's historic Allentown neighborhood serving from-scratch cocktails augmented by a full menu of hors d'oeuvres inspired by cuisines from around the world. The concept allows guests to experience an array of delicious foods, just as one would at an upscale cocktail party. Platters to share and a menu of entrée options round out the modern restaurant's offerings.

Sample received positive reviews upon opening in 2007. In addition, the restaurant has made its mark as a top caterer in the Western New York region, staying busy year-round with events serving from ten to two thousand guests.

Goetz brought an intensity to Nickel City Chef events along with dishes requiring perfect technique and timing. Although not always a winner, his hospitable nature, good sportsmanship, and culinary dexterity has made him an irreplaceable member of the team. Goetz and his sous chef through all three seasons, Chef James Gehrke, made an excellent team.

THE CHEFS

Nickel City Chef Brian Mietus of Bacchus
Season 3

Brian Mietus can trace his love of cooking back to his first experience in the kitchen of his mother's hot dog stand, Curt's Stop In. While attending the New England Culinary Institute, he worked in the kitchen of a restaurant on Nantucket Island before moving to Vail, Colorado. He landed a position in a restaurant named Sweet Basil, and after proving himself to its operators, was promoted to chef de cuisine. While at Sweet Basil, Mietus had the distinction of preparing a James Beard dinner and being featured in *Wine Spectator* magazine.

famed Calumet building, underwent upgrades and remodeling, expanding its private dining facilities and much-loved patio.

Chef Mietus, who lives in Lewiston, New York with his wife and two young children, was the first challenger to compete in the first season, when he beat Nickel City Chef Krista Van Wagner by a single point. So, a season later, when Tempo's Paul Jenkins retired as a Nickel City Chef, Chef Mietus was the obvious replacement.

In 2001 he chose to return to Buffalo and was promptly hired to cook for Oliver's. Chef Mietus was the first chef to earn the esteemed restaurant a four-star review from *The Buffalo News*. In 2005, after a brief stint in the kitchens of Tempo, Mietus assumed the role of executive chef at the new Bacchus Wine Bar & Restaurant. There he installed Buffalo's first menu featuring small plates, and the restaurant earned rave reviews from food critics and a *Wine Spectator* award for its wine list. Two years later he was made managing partner. In 2011 the restaurant, housed in the

Aided by his sous chef, Ronald Rytel, Mietus made an excellent addition to the Nickel City Chef team. Despite his calm exterior he has a passion for competition and loves to win.

Nickel City Chef JJ Richert of Torches
Seasons 1-3

JJ Richert started working in restaurants at the tender age of fifteen as dishwasher for a Western New York country club. After falling in love with the noise and chaotic clatter of the kitchen, he took on extra responsibilities and began to rise through the ranks. Eventually his passion for food prompted him to pursue an education at the Culinary Institute of America in Hyde Park, New York, while returning to Buffalo to work at the country club on weekends. It was at the country club that he met and fell in love with a pastry chef named Cynthia, who eventually would become his wife.

490, a West Side steakhouse, and his brother was named executive chef at Nektar.

But it wasn't long before Chef Richert, his wife, and his brother teamed up to open Torches, a four-star restaurant in Kenmore, New York, that became known for pushing culinary boundaries by employing twists on classic dishes. After four years of success with Torches, the Richert brothers were set to embark on a new venture: Smoke on the Water, a waterfront restaurant in Tonawanda, New York that would showcase their love of speedboats and barbecue.

Upon graduation Richert returned to Buffalo full time to

accept a position as executive chef of Nektar restaurant, where he ultimately hired his brother Kevin as sous chef. Chef JJ Richert went on to open and serve as executive chef for Prime

JJ Richert was the first chef invited to participate in Nickel City Chef, and he graciously served as an advisor during the early planning stages of the event. His penchant for custom motorcycles, tattoos, and rock 'n' roll reveal him as a consummate showman. When his brother Kevin served as sous during competitions, they were a difficult duo to beat. Voted by a local magazine "the chef most deserving of his own television show," JJ Richert brings fire and creativity to every competition.

THE CHEFS

Nickel City Chef Krista Van Wagner of Curly's
Seasons 1-3

A native of South Buffalo, Krista Van Wagner attended the Culinary Institute of America, where she met her future husband, Kirk Van Wagner. After they both graduated, Krista and Kirk traveled the globe, and Krista spent time working in a variety of kitchen positions in locations as diverse as Switzerland and the Caribbean. She also spent time cooking in various regions of the continental U.S.

Eventually she and Kirk returned to Buffalo, where they took over Curly's, a corner bar and grill belonging to Krista's grandfather. A South Buffalo institution serving customers for more than seventy-five years, Curly's was reinvented by the couple as an upscale restaurant, and Van Wagner injected her classical French training and love of Caribbean flavors into a menu otherwise filled with traditional American offerings. It wasn't long before word of her delicious jerk sauce spread, and her line of spicy condiments made its way onto market shelves across the region.

But Van Wagner's passion for the Caribbean goes beyond mere sauces. She is dedicated to providing aid to that corner of the world by volunteering with Jesse's Children, a Western New York organization that sends dentists to the Dominican Republic to provide care to those who cannot afford it. On these missions she acts as an assistant to the dentists. To help fund them, Van Wagner has placed benefit chocolate chip cookies on Curly's menu so that patrons can enjoy warm, spicy treats while contributing to the program. She has also put several Dominican youths through culinary school and even brought them to Buffalo to participate in an externship at her restaurant.

With a family of five, a business, and all of her charity work, it is a wonder Chef Van Wagner had time to be a Nickel City Chef. Perhaps having her husband Kirk as her sous chef helped. She approached each competition with energy and enthusiasm, and on more than one occasion, her worldly palate and deft execution earned her a win.

Nickel City Chef Paul Jenkins of Tempo
Seasons 1-2

Paul Jenkins' first job was tending the grill at a Buffalo hot dog stand. He spent the next twenty-five years cooking in Buffalo's most esteemed restaurants, as well as undertaking a few independent ventures. He honed his craft at Oliver's and Rue Franklin West before becoming the executive chef at the Buffalo Club, where he stayed for many years. Then, in 2005, he joined forces with restaurateur Mark Hutchinson and opened Tempo in a former mansion located on Delaware Avenue's "Millionaires' Row."

Tempo features a sleek and well-appointed dining room coupled with a menu offering fine Mediterranean fare. Jenkins' love of ingredients means that no expense is spared in obtaining the freshest seafood, meats, and produce. Tempo helped breathe new life into the once-struggling downtown Buffalo restaurant scene and proved to be one of the city's most successful restaurants. In 2011 it was named one of the top fifty Italian restaurants in America by *Open Table*, and it is a favorite among visiting celebrities and athletes, as well as Buffalo's elite.

Chef Jenkins has participated in and co-organized "Taste of the Nation" in Buffalo and has annually represented the Buffalo Bills as a "Taste of the NFL" Super Bowl Chef. He is the proud father of two boys and a well-respected leader in Western New York's culinary industry.

In 2009 Jenkins lent his name and abilities to Nickel City Chef. He and his sous chef, Eric Nessa, stayed with the team until 2010, when Jenkins' business development plans to open an oyster bar and eatery with Hutchinson in the newly renovated Remington Lofts in Tonawanda, New York, required his full attention.

THE HOSTS

Host Bert Gambini
Seasons 1-3

Bert Gambini's distinctive voice has been heard on Buffalo radio stations for more than twenty years. He started his career as a news writer and anchor at WHLD in Niagara Falls, New York before moving to a similar position at Buffalo's WBEN. In 1993 he was hired by WBFO to be the local host of National Public Radio's Weekend Edition. Three years later Gambini was named music director, and from 1996 until 2010 he hosted a daily jazz show on

WBFO along with his programming responsibilities.

In 1999 he launched WBFO's Meet the Author series, which brings contemporary nonfiction writers to the Buffalo area. His smooth vocal tones convey news to thousands of Western New York public radio listeners, but his passion for food made him the ideal candidate to host Nickel City Chef.

As a teenager Gambini worked behind the counter at the West Side meat market owned by his father. He knew that the foods he ate at home, like fresh calamari, differed from what graced the dinner tables of his peers. As an adult Gambini has always enjoyed food and cooks for himself and his children. But he recalls a few instances when a dining experience has impacted the way in which he perceived food and dining. One such occasion was at Tsunami, with co-owner Chef Mike Andrzejewski in the kitchen. Gambini cites Andrzejewski for introducing him to sushi and changing the way he thought about fish. Though it was entirely coincidental, Chef Andrzejewski would become Gambini's Nickel City Chef cohost.

Gambini has hosted all sixteen Nickel City challenges, bringing his decades of live radio experience, keen mind, unique ability to turn a phrase, deep dedication to Buffalo's restaurant community, and endless catalog of terrible jokes to every show. His consummate professionalism allowed him to persevere through many trying situations, including power outages, sound problems, unpredictable judges, and breaking his prescription glasses mere seconds before the beginning of a competition. His personality and skills are fundamental to the success of the series.

Host Chef Mike Andrzejewski
Seasons 1-3

Arguably Western New York's most esteemed chef, Mike Andrzejewski has been cooking for as long as he can remember. He made a name for himself at Oliver's by injecting his passion for Asian cookery and fusion into Buffalo's dining scene. He then became a partner in Tsunami, a restaurant widely considered to have fundamentally changed the way Western New Yorkers think about cuisine and what Buffalo has to offer in terms of fine dining. He gained knowledge and experience while traveling the globe, and he, along with his partners, worked to showcase those flavors, textures, and techniques at Tsunami.

In 2005 Andrzejewski was involved in a tragic motorcycle accident that left him unconscious for three weeks. Ultimately, it also cost him most of his left leg, requiring him to use a prosthetic. Recovery involved months of rehabilitation, countless surgeries, and sheer willpower–difficult for the hardiest of souls.

Tsunami eventually closed, and Andrzejewski took advantage of the opportunity to address his mobility challenges by opening a small restaurant, one in which he could reach everything he needed without moving much. Seabar, an intimate restaurant exploring sushi through Andrzejewski's passion for fusion, opened first in Williamsville, New York. The chef's love of seafood and desire to experiment with molecular gastronomy techniques led him to open a second Seabar in downtown Buffalo. It wasn't long before Andrzejewski's mobility improved, and as Seabar blossomed, the talented chef felt limited by the restaurant's diminutive kitchen. A remodel was in order, so he closed the Williamsville location and doubled the size of his Buffalo venue, adding a full kitchen and a large, contemporary dining room. This transformation and his expanded menu earned Seabar rave reviews, including four stars from *The Buffalo News*. Not done yet, Chef Andrzejewski plans to open several more restaurants before 2013.

Despite his busy schedule, he was an early supporter of Nickel City Chef, offering his perspective during the planning stages. Later he brought his vast knowledge of technique and ingredients to the audience by cohosting nearly sixteen competitions, participation that has been crucial to the success of all the events.

THE JUDGES
What's a competition without a winner?

The judges play an essential role in Nickel City Chef, and choosing them is a difficult process. Prime parameters include an understanding of general gastronomy, objectivity, excellent credentials, and... personality. Delivering witty, insightful, and genuine commentary after having time to taste only one or two quick bites of a dish is no small task.

A core team of professionals made up of die-hard foodies, trained culinarians, and food writers, sits at the judges' table every season. They are augmented by a number of guest judges. Although the food is often delicious, telling a chef in front of a live audience about the shortcomings of a dish is difficult, particularly after witnessing the effort that went into it in the mad dash of competition. Without a panel of qualified and entertaining judges, Nickel City Chef wouldn't be fair, and it certainly wouldn't be much fun.

Kristen Becker
Comedienne, Buffalo, NY

Becker's bawdy humor has earned her national recognition as a performer and producer. As the founder of the *Dykes of Hazard Comedy Tour*, she has toured venues across the nation, and her *Doin' Time Comedy* has caused a resurgence in Buffalo's comedy scene. Becker's appreciation for well-prepared food and thoughtful flavor profiles can be traced back to the years she spent working as a manager in the restaurants of New Orleans, Louisiana. Her knowledgeable commentary, richly spiced with her own brand of humor, have regaled Nickel City Chef audiences.

Alan Bedenko
Restaurant Critic, Buffalo, NY

Alan Bedenko is an attorney and the voice behind one of Buffalo's best-known blogs, *Buffalo Pundit*. In 2004 his love of good dining and opinionated writing led to a position as a restaurant critic at Western New York's premier magazine, *Buffalo Spree*. Bedenko is a stickler, particularly regarding technical preparation and authenticity. His bold personality and critical nature make him one tough judge.

John Bourdage
Food and Wine Consultant, Buffalo, NY

As a graduate of Ivor Spencer School for Butler Administration, Bourdage received training in manners, etiquette, food and wine, entertaining, and the fine arts. His practice calls on him to share his experiences, including the improvement of interpersonal relationships through a renewed understanding of service and social skills. This lofty perspective on the Nickel City Chef fare has enriched and enhanced the challenges.

Ivy Knight
Chef and Food Writer, Toronto, ON

With ten years of experience cooking in professional kitchens, Knight's approach to writing is from a cook's perspective. In just five years as a freelance writer, she has seen her work appear in many publications, among them the *Globe and Mail, Toronto Life*, the *Toronto Star* and *eGullet*. Knight is knowledgeable, articulate, and insightful, the hallmarks of a good judge.

Mary Luz Mejia
Food Writer and Television Producer, Toronto, ON

A journalist, researcher and Canadian Gemini award-nominated food television producer, Mejia has traveled to twenty-eight countries (and counting) in the course of her work. She is currently the contributing editor of the culinary tourism section for *Ensemble Vacations*. Her international experience with both food and entertainment has made her an invaluable voice on the panel of judges.

Don Salamone
Executive Sous Chef, San Francisco, CA

Salamone began his cooking career in the private clubs of Western New York. After making the Dean's List at the Western Culinary Institute in Portland, Oregon, he has worked in the kitchens of Guy Savoy, Gordon Ramsay, Joel Robuchon, and most recently as executive sous chef for Michael Mina. He brings a rich West Coast perspective to his hometown culinary scene.

Nelson Starr
Musician, Buffalo, NY

Buffalo Music Hall of Fame member and rocker Nelson Starr is best known as one of Buffalo's influential musicians, composers, and producers. Recently he has focused his acumen on the culinary world. In addition to having brought celebrity chef and Travel Channel star Anthony Bourdain to Buffalo, Starr now also hosts his own hit online food series, *All Access Pass*.

THE SPONSORS

If it takes a village to raise a child, it takes an entire region to bring to fruition a project the size of Nickel City Chef. Among the many organizations that provide the support needed to produce a project of this scope four stand out.

Artisan Kitchens & Baths

The opportunity to run a public event in a location as beautiful and well equipped as Artisan Kitchens & Baths is pleasure enough, but working with a team of creative thinkers with a positive attitude who also appreciate the importance of customer service has been particularly delightful. With the full support of Vice President Kevin Telaak, the Artisan Kitchen & Baths personnel are quick to share their diverse abilities, and their dedication to Buffalo and its heritage are notable. Allowing us use of their state-of-the-art, one-of-a-kind facility spurred the creation of Nickel City Chef, but their friendship, generosity, and hospitable nature are what have encouraged us to continue producing competitions season after season.

The Mansion on Delaware Avenue

The Mansion on Delaware Avenue is the finest boutique hotel in Western New York. Located along "Millionaires' Row" on Delaware Avenue in Buffalo, the formerly abandoned Second Empire-style building was lovingly and tastefully resurrected by Geno and Diana Principe. After years of extensive restoration work, the hotel opened in 2001, quickly garnering acclaim from Zagat, Frommer's, and the American Automobile Association (AAA). The Principes have been long time supporters of Feed Your Soul and its efforts to highlight the most talented chefs and ingredients in Western New York. What better way to introduce a visiting judge to Buffalo than to tuck them into this unique and well-appointed luxury hotel? Introducing guests to Buffalo's world-class architecture and hospitality at the hands of the extraordinary staff of The Mansion on Delaware Avenue has been a point of pride for the Nickel City Chef team.

The Mansion's chef and staff have also provided Nickel City Chef with excellent catering services, a delicious privilege typically reserved for those fortunate enough to attend one of the hotel's private parties.

Wegmans

Wegmans is a Western New York institution. This award-winning supermarket chain is dedicated to providing customers with locally raised produce, ingredients from around the globe, and unparalleled customer service, combined with a strong commitment to the community. In the week prior to a competition, the Nickel City Chef staff combs through the Amherst Street store for the freshest and most exciting ingredients to replenish the Wegmans' Market Pantry. This well-stocked pantry of more than two hundred fresh and dry grocery items stands at the center of each Nickel City Chef competition.

Offering the chefs the superior ingredients found in the aisles of Wegmans provides each of them with the opportunity to do their best work. Wegmans' support of Nickel City Chef has been invaluable. Staff, chefs, and executives alike have provided Nickel City Chef with the consistent service that has become synonymous with the Wegmans' name.

CUTCO Cutlery

CUTCO is located in the Allegheny foothills of Olean, New York, where it has been producing cutlery since 1949. The company traces its roots back to skilled cutlers who settled in the area, immigrating from England's famous Sheffield cutlery industry in the late 1800s. Today its factory and Visitors Center employ more than 400 Western New Yorkers. Nickel City Chef's strong belief in supporting local businesses and artisans make its partnership with CUTCO a perfect match. CUTCO knives are the only ones still made entirely in the United States. A CUTCO knife's durable and exceptionally sharp edge, patented handle grip, and lifetime guarantee make it a useful tool for professional kitchens and home cooks. Full sets of Cutco knives outfit both of Nickel City Chef's competition kitchens, and our chefs couldn't be happier. Also very pleased is the fortunate Nickel City Chef fan who returns home from each challenge with a set of beautiful CUTCO knives.

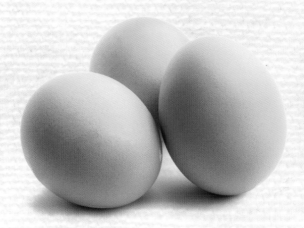

CHALLENGE 1

Eggs

FROM KREHER'S FARM

 VS.

Nickel City Chef
Krista Van Wagner
Curly's, Lackawanna, NY

Challenging Chef
Brian Mietus
Bacchus, Buffalo, NY

Kreher's Farm
Clarence, New York

Kreher's Farm, located in Clarence, New York, produces eggs for Eggland's Best Eggs.

The chicken egg is one of those fascinating foodstuffs that we all take for granted. Perhaps because eggs are such an ubiquitous part of our ordinary, day-to-day lives, we often fail to marvel at just how amazing they really are.

With more than eighty years of egg farming under their belts, the folks at Kreher's Farm are certainly comfortable with the little white orbs, and time has not diminished their passion for a good egg. Kreher's Farm eggs were the first Nickel City Chef secret ingredient, and made an ideal opener to the series.

Kreher's Farm is owned by seven members of the Kreher family. The farm began in 1924, before being passed down to the second generation in 1950, and then to its current owners in 1992. The family has consistently worked to ensure that the eggs produced on its farm are as delicious and nutritious as possible, and the present-day owners take great pride in implementing environmentally friendly policies that will help extend their legacy to future generations. As Scott Kreher puts it, "We want to supply a top-of-the-line product, while preserving the land that my grandparents began working more than eighty years ago, so that future generations of our family can carry on the tradition."

So what is that top-of-the-line product? Quite simply, it's a mighty fine egg. Kreher's Farm is an Eggland's Best Eggs franchisee, which means it uses a patented chicken feed to produce Eggland's Best Eggs. This is an all-natural and all-vegetarian diet, containing grains, canola oil, rice bran, alfalfa, sea kelp, and Vitamin E. The Kreher family staunchly believes that the quality of eggs it currently produces is the highest in the farm's long history.

The unique composition of the Eggland's Best patented chicken feed can lead to some interesting outcomes. For example, each egg contains ten times more Vitamin E than one produced by a chicken that eats a less-specialized, more ordinary feed. And, most important to those of us consuming the product, good feed leads to tastier eggs.

By partnering with Eggland's Best, the Krehers have been able to continue to run a local family business while simultaneously improving the quality and distribution of their eggs throughout the region. Kreher's Farm has also implemented an extensive composting system on the family farm in Clarence. "The waste from our hens is collected and transported to two composting buildings using a conveyor belt system," says Scott Kreher. "Some of the compost is sold to local organic farmers as organic fertilizer with high nitrogen value. Along with our laying facilities, we also have 3,000 acres of our own organic crops, so much of the compost goes right back into our land."

C. S. Lewis once said, "No clever arrangement of bad eggs ever made a good omelet." This is true in both a metaphoric and literal sense, since a bad egg is a rotten starting point for any cook. Luckily, Kreher's Farm and Eggland's Best Eggs ensure that we have access to high quality, tasty eggs. And that led to the presentation of some pretty spectacular dishes by both chefs during the first Nickel City Chef challenge.

Planning for the first Nickel City Chef competition was a nerve-wracking and harrowing experience for the event's production staff. There was no way to be sure that every nuance of the show had been considered and properly prepared for until the crew had produced at least one live show.

Fortunately, two of the most professional chefs in the area were slated to compete that day. With Krista Van Wagner of Curly's in the Nickel City Chef kitchen, the audience was not only able to see an experienced and confident chef at work, but Van Wagner's shining personality and winning smile set everyone at ease. The challenging chef was Brian Mietus of Bacchus, who would eventually become a Nickel City Chef himself in the third season of the series. (At the time, the crew had no idea that future seasons would be an option!)

"To those with culinary knowledge who had been able to carefully watch every move Chef Van Wagner made, it was clear she had pushed herself to use the egg in every imaginable way."

It was clear from the start that Mietus had tremendous respect for Van Wagner and was, in his own right, a solid competitor; he had already won several cooking competitions over the course of his career. In fact, the production staff credits the professionalism, good sportsmanship, and level-headedness of these two chefs for setting the tone and level of excellence for the entire series.

The Buffalo News published a nice article about the new Nickel City Chef competition, and tickets for the first season sold out in just a few days. The panel of judges: *Buffalo Spree* magazine restaurant critic Alan Bedenko, comedienne Kristen Becker, and wine enthusiast Kevin LoVullo, were treated to six dishes featuring the marvelous and wonderful egg.

During the portion of the show in which each chef presents his or her dishes to the judges for tasting, the Nickel City Chef staff learned a valuable lesson. In every dish, Challenger Mietus' use of the egg was apparent–ribbons of egg graced his niçoise, a fried egg topped his carpaccio, and his egg custard course was served in an open egg shell.

But Nickel City Chef Van Wagner, who had used the egg in myriad ways–in a sauce, as a crêpe for the wrapper and as a binder for the stuffing of her "egg roll," in a vinaigrette, and as a mousse–failed to convey all of these methods to the panel and the audience. She instead simply told the judges the names of her dishes.

To those with culinary knowledge who had been able to carefully watch every move Chef Van Wagner made, it was clear she had pushed herself to use the egg in every way imaginable. But early on in Nickel City Chef, the judges did not sit on a raised dais, and there was not yet a live, roving camera in each kitchen, beaming lush food imagery onto flat-panel televisions mounted throughout the viewing area. Therefore, the judges missed this aspect of Van Wagner's performance, and she was penalized in the points she was awarded for the category in which the judges determine how well each chef has used the secret ingredient.

Mietus' dishes were expertly crafted, restrained, and beautiful. He impressed everyone and deserved the win, but from this point on, the Nickel City Chef staff worked to help each chef–whether a Nickel City Chef or a Challenger–understand how vitally important it was that the tableside presentation convey information about technique, concept, and execution to both the judges and the audience.

Nickel City Chef Brian Mietus, executive chef and managing partner of Bacchus restaurant, sears foie gras for his third course.

Nancy J. Parisi

CHALLENGING CHEF BRIAN MIETUS'

Tuna Niçoise

Servings: 6 | Total prep and cooking time: 45 minutes

INGREDIENTS

1 pound sushi-grade Ahi tuna

2 red or yellow bell peppers

1/4 pound haricot vert

6 egg whites

2 large Russet potatoes

1 cup grape tomatoes, halved

1/4 cup Kalamata olives, pitted

1/4 pound baby arugula

4 cloves garlic, minced

1 medium shallot, minced

4 tablespoons red wine vinegar

6 tablespoons extra virgin olive oil

12 large basil leaves

Salt and pepper

DIRECTIONS

• Roast the red peppers over an open flame. Allow them to cool for a moment. Using paper towels (but being careful not to burn yourself), wipe away the peel. Leave the peppers to cool; then slice and reserve.

• Blanch the green beans, and shock them in an ice water bath. Drain and reserve.

• In a small bowl, combine the garlic, shallot, tomatoes, red wine vinegar, and extra virgin olive oil. Set aside. Each of these steps can be done in advance.

• Peel the potatoes and spin them on a turning slicer, producing a large curl of potato.

• Wrap the curls around the Ahi tuna, leaving a double layer of potato. Heat a sauté pan. Add a small amount of oil. Sear the tuna, until it is golden brown on all sides.

• Beat the egg white lightly and season with salt. Add a thin layer of eggs to a hot sauté pan, creating an egg "crêpe." Fold and turn out onto a cutting board. When cool to the touch, slice the egg "crêpe" into fettuccine-like strands.

• Toss the egg whites, haricot vert, peppers, basil, olives, and arugula in the sherry vinaigrette. Season with salt and pepper.

PLATING

Gently heap salad into the center of a plate and top with a slice of potato-crusted tuna.

CHALLENGE 1: EGGS FROM KREHER'S FARM

NICKEL CITY CHEF KRISTA VAN WAGNER'S
Rib Eye
with Sherry Saffron Aioli, Fiddleheads, and Fingerling Potato Salad

Nancy J. Parisi

Servings: 4 | Total prep and cooking time: 1 hour | Preheat oven to 375°F

INGREDIENTS

2 cloves garlic, minced
1/2 teaspoon kosher salt
1 egg yolk
1 lemon, juiced
1 cup extra virgin olive oil
8 saffron threads
Salt and pepper

DIRECTIONS

Saffron Aioli
• Place garlic and salt in food processor. Pulse for two seconds. Add egg yolk and lemon juice, pulsing until blended. Turn food processor on medium speed and add olive oil in a thin stream until combined. Finish with saffron and pepper (salt if needed).

---

1 pound fingerling potatoes
1/4 pound bacon, diced
1 medium onion, diced
1 teaspoon flour
12 ounces sherry vinegar
2 ounces New York honey
Salt and white pepper
8 ounces grape seed oil
(or other lightly flavored oil)

Fingerling Potato Salad
• Clean potatoes and cook in salted boiling water until fork tender. Drain and cool. Slice in half lengthwise and reserve.

• Place bacon in a skillet over medium heat and cook until almost crisp. Remove bacon to drain on a paper towel. Add onion to bacon fat and cook until translucent. Remove onion from pan, reserving fat. Drain off all but one tablespoon of bacon fat.

• Over medium heat, add flour and brown lightly. Mix in sherry, vinegar, honey, and salt and pepper to taste. Whisk in oil. Pour hot dressing over potatoes.

---

4 rib eye steaks of good quality
Kosher salt and fresh ground pepper

Rib Eye Steaks
• Season steaks with salt and pepper on all sides. Transfer seasoned steaks to the hot sauté pan and cook until desired doneness. Let stand 5 to 10 minutes before slicing.

---

1 cup fiddlehead ferns
2 cloves garlic, chopped
2 tablespoons unsalted butter
Salt and pepper

Fiddleheads
• Boil cleaned fiddleheads in salted water for 5 minutes. Strain and shock in a cold water bath. Strain and reserve.

• Heat butter and garlic in a sauté pan until fragrant. Add fiddleheads to pan and toss. Season with salt and pepper. Serve warm.

PLATING
Use a long, narrow plate for this dish. On one end, pool 3 tablespoons of saffron aioli onto the plate, topping it with freshly sautéed fiddleheads. Place a portion of fingerling potatoes on the opposite end of the plate, adding several slices of warm steak in between.

Chef's notes
If you are unable to locate fiddleheads, which are in season only for a brief time in spring, the best substitution is asparagus. For ease of preparation, complete the aioli recipe and boil the fiddleheads and potatoes ahead of time. One hour before serving, remove these items from the refrigerator and finish them. First, put the steaks on, then cook the bacon for the potatoes, making the warm vinaigrette for the potato salad. Then, while the steaks are resting, warm the fiddleheads by cooking them in the garlic butter and the potatoes by tossing them in the vinaigrette. Aioli should be at served at room temperature.

CHALLENGE 1: EGGS FROM KREHER'S FARM

CHALLENGING CHEF
Brian Mietus
of Bacchus Restaurant

Tuna Niçoise
Potato-encrusted Tuna Steak, Egg, Haricot Vert, Roasted Red Peppers, Niçoise Olives

Steak & Eggs
Seasoned Beef Carpacccio, Poached Egg, Truffle

Egg Custard with Foie Gras

NICKEL CITY CHEF
Krista Van Wagner
of Curly's

Dry-aged Rib Eye
Saffron Aioli, Sautéed Fiddleheads, Fingerling Potatoes, Aged Sherry Egg Vinaigrette

Crispy Egg Roll
Shrimp Mousse, Lavender Cream

Strawberry Zabaglione
Passion Fruit Gelée, Coconut Caviar, Pistachios

SCORES FOR CHALLENGE 1

	Challenging Chef Brian Mietus		Nickel City Chef Krista Van Wagner
Taste & Flavor	11	Taste & Flavor	11
Creativity	11	Creativity	11
Plating & Presentation	10	Plating & Presentation	12
Technical Execution	11	Technical Execution	10
Use of Secret Ingredient	11	Use of Secret Ingredient	8
Audience Vote	0	Audience Vote	1
Total	**54**		**53**

Nancy J. Parisi

The Challenger:
Chef Brian Mietus
Bacchus Restaurant
56 West Chippewa, Buffalo
ultimaterestaurants.com/bacchus

Brian Mietus attended the New England Culinary Institute. After graduation, he spent time working in the kitchen of a restaurant on Nantucket Island before moving to Vail. There he found a position at Sweet Basil, a well-regarded restaurant. He was ultimately promoted to the role of chef de cuisine.

In 2001, Chef Mietus returned to Buffalo. Landing a position at the venerable Oliver's, he was the first chef to earn the restaurant a four-star review from *The Buffalo News*. In 2005, Mietus was named executive chef of Bacchus Wine Bar & Restaurant. Two years later he was made managing partner. Today, Bacchus is well recognized for its consistency and quality, excellent service, and thoughtful wine list.

> He was the first chef to earn Oliver's restaurant a four-star review from *The Buffalo News*.

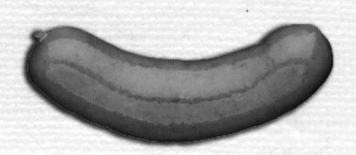

CHALLENGE 2

Sausage

FROM SPAR'S EUROPEAN SAUSAGE

 VS.

Nickel City Chef
JJ Richert
Torches
Kenmore, NY

Challenging Chef
Joseph Fenush III
Park Country Club
Williamsville, NY

Spar's European Sausage and Meats

Buffalo, New York   sparseuropeansausage.com

Spar's European Sausage and Meats is a Buffalo icon. It has done steady business in the Grant-Amherst neighborhood for decades, first under the watchful eye of German-born Eric Spar, and more recently at the careful hands of Joe Kennedy and his wife, Beth. Sausages from Spar's were an appropriate choice as the secret ingredient for Nickel City Chef's second challenge.

Spar opened the shop in the late 1980s and it quickly became a local favorite, producing good quality sausages of Buffalo's favorite sort—Italian, Polish, and German. In 2002, Joe Kennedy, a chef looking for a career change, came to apprentice under Spar. In two years, the shop's namesake imparted a lifetime of experience to the eager chef. Feeling confident that his legacy would not be lost, Spar sold the business to the Kennedys in 2005.

With the skills and techniques learned during his apprenticeship and the recipes he inherited from Spar, Kennedy could have continued to run this successful neighborhood business as it was. Instead, his natural creativity and culinary background inspired him to expand beyond the shop's original product line. Today, Spar's consistently stocks more than forty varieties of sausage, both fresh and smoked. Chorizo, andouille, English bangers, and Calabrese sausages now line the glass butcher's case, nestled beside the classic Polish- and Italian-style delights that have been a part of the Buffalo diet for more than a century.

Kennedy's creativity knows no bounds. Chicken, pork, and lamb sausages inspired by cultures from all over the world are available, as are those that seem to come directly from Kennedy's imagination, such as the pork and sweet potato sausage, or a Buffalo wing-inspired chicken sausage. Many are sold fresh, ready for the stovetop or grill. Others are smoked, using the ancient wood smoker located in the working area of the shop. This irreplaceable piece of equipment is carefully tended, having produced millions of smoked sausages over many decades, imbuing Spar's smoked meats with remarkable flavor and amazing character. Kennedy's commitment to using the best ingredients and timeworn techniques shines through whether the meats are smoked or fresh.

"Sausage has been elevated," says Kennedy. "It's an ancient art that started out as food for the poverty class—a way for people to do the best they could with as little as possible. Today, it's entirely different." Consider that Spar's sausages now appear on the menus of many of Buffalo's finest dining establishments. During one visit, no fewer than three chefs dressed in whites came through the door, each representing a reputable eatery, each willing to make a special trip to pick up some of the best sausage in Western New York.

Nickel City Chef's second battle featured four types of Spar's sausage: a classic beer-enhanced bratwurst, fresh Merguez (a spicy Moroccan sausage made of ground lamb), and two smoked sausages—andouille and chorizo. These are favorites among Spar's regular customers.

From the abundance of sausage varieties and the deli case laden with European luncheon meats and cheeses, to the specialty foods shelves bursting with imported goods, the variety and quality of the tiny shop's products are unparalleled. Spar's is an asset to its neighborhood, luring visitors with the promise of remarkable edibles found nowhere else in the area.

Joe Kennedy displays freshly made links in his workroom, just a few feet from Spar's famous smoker.

The chefs chosen for the second challenge could not have been more different. During this competition, Nickel City Chef JJ Richert revealed why the restaurant he owns with his brother Kevin is called Torches. This maverick used a variety of heat sources to prepare his three courses, including a charcoal grill. The scent of burning charcoal filled the showroom as the chef and his sous produced dishes using classic cooking techniques devised to highlight the individual quality of each sausage's cultural heritage.

Those familiar with Torches appreciate the restaurant's simple, straightforward cooking enhanced by imaginative twists. The Richert brothers surprised everyone by staying true to the roots of each type of sausage that Spar's brought to the table.

The young and eager challenger, Joseph Fenush III, who was at the time the *chef de cuisine* at Williamsville's Park Country Club, took a number of risks with a bold menu. He employed modern cooking techniques that featured the use of liquid nitrogen and other chemical-based preparations most often associated with molecular gastronomy. With classic technique on one side of the stage and modern cooking on the other, this battle of fire and ice was the most exciting competition of Nickel City Chef's first season.

"With classic technique on one side of the stage and modern cooking on the other, this battle of fire and ice was the most exciting competition of Nickel City Chef's first season."

The panel of judges included Joe and Beth Kennedy, the owners of Spar's European Sausage and the makers of the day's secret ingredient. That led to a second well-learned lesson about how to cook for a panel of judges: Many artisan food makers do not appreciate seeing their food toyed with!

Joe and Beth are dedicated and talented food producers with a true passion for what they do. They were disturbed to see their smoked sausages being charred, or worse yet, frozen with liquid nitrogen and shaved into wafer thin slices. However, as a *chef de cuisine* at several area fine-dining restaurants before purchasing Spar's, Joe Kennedy also appreciated the skills and techniques the chefs were demonstrating, and he returned to Nickel City Chef as a sous chef to challenger Dino DeBell of Blue Monk in the second season.

But despite Kennedy's understanding of the time restrictions imposed during the competition and the abilities of the chefs involved, he felt that the very nature of his artisanally crafted sausage had been compromised, and this was certainly reflected in the way in which he voted. We learned to limit the occasions on which a food producer was invited to be a judge, not because they aren't qualified, but because of their emotional attachment to their product. Our chefs may unintentionally offend in their drive to really explore an ingredient.

LEI Photography

Challenging Chef Fenush and his sous, Daniel Lawrence, double-check their equipment list before the audience arrives.

CHALLENGE 2: SAUSAGE FROM SPAR'S EUROPEAN SAUSAGE

CHALLENGING CHEF FENUSH'S
Shrimp and Grits

Servings: 6 | Total prep and cooking time: 2 hours | Preheat oven to 300° F

INGREDIENTS

12 large shrimp, shell on

8 ears of corn

2 links Spar's smoked andouille sausage

2 quarts stock (light lobster, chicken, pork, or vegetable)

1 large onion, diced

4 cloves garlic, roughly chopped

3 bay leaves

1/4 pound cold unsalted butter, cubed

2 limes, juiced and zested

Tabasco

Salt

FOR GARNISH

Watercress leaves

Parsley leaves

Cilantro leaves

Coriander seed, toasted and coarsely ground

LEI Photography

DIRECTIONS

• Slice one and a half links of andouille sausage into very thin slices. Place approximately 20 slices in a single layer on a sheet pan and cook in the oven until dry and crispy–about 30 minutes. Place the remaining half link into the freezer. Any remaining slices or scraps should be put into a heavy-bottomed pot with the stock, onion, garlic, and bay leaf.

• Cook broth for 60 minutes over medium heat.

• Cut kernels away from the corn cobs, then scrape the cob with a spoon, reserving all juices and pulp. Cook the corn kernels and pulp over medium heat in a saucepan for 45 minutes, or until mixture has thickened. Stir in the butter, lime juice, and Tabasco and salt to taste. Once combined, remove from heat and cover to keep warm.

• While the corn is thickening, use a sharp knife to devein the shrimp, leaving the shells on. Once the broth has fortified, poach the shrimp until firm, about 3 to 5 minutes. Remove the shrimp and allow to cool.

• Strain broth into smaller, clean saucepan and continue to reduce.

• Once shrimp are cool enough to handle, peel and reserve in cooler. Chop or tear shrimp into bite-sized pieces. This step can be done ahead of time, with shrimp rewarmed gently in a sauté pan with butter.

PLATING

In a large, shallow dish, spoon the fresh corn grits in the center. Place shrimp and crispy andouille alternately along one side. Pour a little broth around grits. Using a microplane, grate the frozen andouille link as a garnish, forming a fluffy, dusty layer over the grits. Randomly place watercress, parsley, and cilantro leaves, and season with salt, lime zest, and coarsely ground, toasted coriander seed.

Chef's notes

This is really a warm-weather recipe, since it calls for fresh corn, but in North America, most great shrimp are available in the colder months. So feel free to make this recipe in winter using traditional stone-ground grits and maybe a stock made from summer corn cobs frozen for a little seasonal nostalgia. You can also make the grits using leftover corn bread ground into crumbs and cooked like traditional grits with the stock of your choice.

NICKEL CITY CHEF JJ RICHERT'S

Gnocchi with Merguez
and Sundried Tomato Pesto

Nancy J. Parisi

Servings: 4 | Total prep and cooking time: 1 hour | Preheat oven to 375°F

INGREDIENTS

4 Russet potatoes, peeled and
  cut into 1-inch cubes

1 egg

1/4 cup grated Parmesan

1/4 teaspoon ground nutmeg

4 cups 00 Italian flour

4 Spar's fresh Merguez sausage

1/2 cup fresh basil leaves

4 cloves garlic

1 teaspoon lemon zest

1/4 teaspoon coarse salt

1 cup sundried tomatoes in oil

1/4 cup grated Parmesan

1 cup olive oil

DIRECTIONS

Potato Gnocchi

• Boil the potatoes in salted water until tender and drain.

• Rice the boiled potatoes in a food mill. Add the egg, Parmesan, and nutmeg. Combine. Work the flour into the mixture, one cup at a time, until the dough begins to pull away from the sides of the bowl.

• Turn out onto a floured board and mix by hand until dough is soft, yet workable. Roll into 1-inch ropes, using a sharp knife to slice each roll into 1-inch pieces. Let pieces set for 15 minutes. Cook the gnocchi in boiling salted water until they float. Pull off and place briefly in an ice bath to arrest temperature. Once cooled, drain and oil lightly. Reserve.

Sundried Tomato Pesto

• Drain the tomatoes and pat dry with a paper towel. Place basil, garlic, lemon zest, and salt in a large food processor. Process until coarsely chopped. Add the sundried tomatoes and Parmesan, processing until the tomatoes are coarsely chopped. Stream in the olive oil slowly, continuing to process until the pesto comes together.

• Grill or pan cook the Merguez sausage, being careful not to overcook. Add the pesto and gnocchi, warming through.

PLATING

This dish is best served family style. Heap the gnocchi on a large white platter, lay the sausage links on top, and drizzle the entire dish with pesto.

LEI Photography

CHALLENGE 2: SAUSAGE FROM SPAR'S EUROPEAN SAUSAGE

22

CHALLENGING CHEF
Joseph Fenush III
of Park Country Club

Sausage Degustation

Deconstructed Shrimp and Grits

Celebration of Summer Vegetables

NICKEL CITY CHEF
JJ Richert
of Torches

German Beer Brat
Caraway-scented Sauerkraut,
Spaetzle, and Beer

Traditional Paella
Andouille-stuffed Calamari

Grilled Merguez Sausage
Handmade Gnocchi,
Sundried Tomato and
Basil Pesto

SCORES FOR CHALLENGE 2

Challenging Chef Joseph Fenush III		Nickel City Chef JJ Richert	
Taste & Flavor	9	Taste & Flavor	10
Creativity	12	Creativity	10
Plating & Presentation	11	Plating & Presentation	12
Technical Execution	8	Technical Execution	9
Use of Secret Ingredient	7	Use of Secret Ingredient	12
Audience Vote	0	Audience Vote	1
Total	**47**		**54**

The Challenger:
Chef Joseph Fenush III
Park Country Club
4949 Sheridan Drive, Williamsville
parkclub.org

You could say that Joseph Fenush grew up at Park Country Club, having spent a large part of his young adult life employed there. This opportunity allowed him to experience every aspect of the club's extensive and busy kitchen, and as he learned, he grew, eventually becoming the *chef de cuisine*.

Now employed as a sous chef at the Southern Hills Country Club in Tulsa, Oklahoma, Fenush's kitchen serves several dining rooms. He hopes his next job will take him to a hotel kitchen in Europe or Asia, ultimately providing him with the kind of experience he feels he needs to return to Western New York and open a restaurant—or two—of his own.

Describing his style as "eclectic," Fenush's skills are rooted in time-honored tradition but include modern techniques and the analytical nature of science; he is inspired by anything and everything. "The challenge of being a great chef," Fenush says, "is that, at any given moment, you are a craftsman, artist, physicist, chemist, politician, psychologist, engineer, and more."

> **Fenush's skills are rooted in time-honored tradition but open to modern techniques.**

CHALLENGE 3

Yogurt

FROM WHITE COW DAIRY

VS.

Nickel City Chef
Paul Jenkins
Tempo
Buffalo, NY

Challenging Chef
Bruce Wieszala
Verbena Grille
Williamsville, NY

White Cow Dairy

East Otto, New York   whitecowdairy.com

With White Cow Dairy's use of traditional recipes, locally sourced ingredients, and small-batch production methods, it comes as no surprise that *Saveur* magazine, Slow Food USA, and other distinguished culinary organizations have recognized the company's artisanal yogurt products. Nickel City Chef recognized it, too, choosing White Cow yogurt as a secret ingredient during the competition's debut season.

The company is the brainchild of Western New York food visionary Patrick Lango, a man with farming in his blood. The owners of a fourth-generation dairy farm in the Town of Boston, Lango's family began raising grass-fed beef after his father passed away, but eventually returned to dairying.

Lango had left the farm years before to work elsewhere, returning home in the 1980s. Soon his family relocated to 250 acres of rolling meadowland and forest in East Otto–Blue Hill Farm. They quickly discovered that the business of selling milk had changed drastically over the decades; economies of scale were forcing small dairies like theirs out of business as the industry demanded higher volumes and lower prices.

Lango needed a solution to keep the farm going. Research in Italy on slow food culture and trips to New York City convinced him that switching to handcrafted dairy products would appeal to food lovers hungry for something different. It was a financial decision, but one that also sought to preserve and celebrate small-scale farming, with healthy cows and farming practices attuned to nature and high-quality products, and Lango's family at its center.

"I fought the system and worked with a dairy cooperative for a long time, and I'm glad for that," Lango says. "But how do you survive and raise a family in this wonderful setting?" The answer, he discovered, was "to go around it, above it, and underneath it. You have to make food."

Lango began to experiment with traditional nineteenth-century American dairy recipes, testing out butters and cheeses. Then came an epiphany–he discovered yogurt. It was versatile, nutritious, and delicious, and wasted far less milk than cheese-making.

He tested his first batch of yogurt at a few local retail outlets and at Murray's, New York City's legendary cheese shop. The response was so overwhelming that the family installed a licensed kitchen on the farm, and in 2007 White Cow Dairy, LLC was born.

To capture the simplicity and authenticity of a less industrialized food system, White Cow purposely keeps its methods traditional and its output small. Lango transforms Blue Hill's milk into yogurt eight feet away from the milking barn. The farm's hillside pasture reaches nearly 1,800 feet in elevation, and the seasons are distinct, supplying the herd with an ever-changing diet of native flowers, weeds, and grasses. Coltsfoot, burdock, violet and fescue, peppermint, nettle, buttercup, and clover grow naturally, giving the milk a taste you simply can't find anywhere else.

Each season, Lango experiments with new flavor combinations and ingredients found a stone's throw away from his kitchen. Yogurts and caramels are made with a touch of New York maple syrup gathered and boiled from nearby forests. In the spring, Lango might choose wild leeks one week, rhubarb or fresh tarragon the next. Locally grown chiles, blueberries, apples, pumpkin, and butternut squash also find their way into the signature White Cow recycled-glass jars.

Today, Murray's, several Western New York farmers' markets, and Wegmans supermarkets carry White Cow's custards, thick yogurts, sauces, and whey-based dairy drinks. Fine restaurants in Buffalo and beyond use the crème fraîche, as well as the luscious, rose-water-tinged Crème Bulgare. Lango's plain yogurt, heavy cream, and quark, a soft German-style cheese with a mild flavor, were featured in Nickel City Chef's third Challenge.

White Cow's success, Lango stresses, goes back to the reason his family started farming in the first place. "Its really about bringing out the character of the milk. If you start with great milk, you'll get great food." As any White Cow fan can attest, "great" might be putting it mildly—let's call it extraordinary.

Patrick Lango, known as the "Willy Wonka of yogurt," uses the milk from his 27 grass-fed cows to create dairy products that have impressed many of the country's culinary elite.

In the third competition of the first season, Paul Jenkins of Tempo, one of Buffalo's most established and well-respected chefs, made his debut as a Nickel City Chef. His participation in the series, along with that of guest host Mike Andrzejewski, gave Nickel City Chef the credibility it required to be considered a serious competition by our dedicated restaurant community.

The room was electric with nervous energy even before the chefs had been introduced. Chef Jenkins has a serious following, and tickets to this show had sold with lightning speed. Challenging Chef Bruce Wieszala was something of a prodigal son, having returned to Buffalo after a decade away in Atlanta. There, he had cooked with several of that city's finest chefs, learning how to butcher meat and focusing on seasonal cooking using Atlanta's brimming farmers markets to keep his kitchen well-stocked. The contrast of putting one of Buffalo's more venerable and well-established chefs up against a new, up-and-coming chef was appealing.

In addition, being able to feature White Cow Dairy's products as a secret ingredient was an honor. All of our secret ingredients are special and interesting in their own way, since all are grown or created by people with tremendous passion for what they do and a real dedication to Western New York. But White Cow Dairy offers an ingredient that is unique, not only to our area, but to the country.

Some call this yogurt "European-style" because of its thickness and quality, but the truth is White Cow Dairy's yogurts are Western New York through and through. It is the *terroir* (a wine term used to describe how the soils, climate, wind, and geographical location of a vineyard influence the flavor of the grape) of Blue Hill Farm that fills this yogurt with flavor and complexity. Lango's goal to manipulate the product as little as possible, flavoring it only with fresh ingredients found within proximity of his farm, means that every jar is a joy, redolent of nature's bounty.

"The contrast of putting one of Buffalo's more venerable and well-established chefs up against a new, up-and-coming chef was appealing."

As with our second challenge, the producer of the secret ingredient was asked to be a judge. Patrick Lango and his fellow judges, Elizabeth Licata, editor-in-chief of *Buffalo Spree* magazine, and Andrew Galarneau, food writer for *The Buffalo News*, were treated to six courses featuring several White Cow products. The two chefs approached their menus very differently, revealing just how fascinating and versatile White Cow Dairy's products can be.

Nickel City Chef Paul Jenkins took a worldly approach, featuring a Lebanese first course, an Italian second course, and an American third course. Challenger Wieszala played largely with Mediterranean preparations.

Nickel City Chef Jenkins and challenger Chef Wieszala load up with the secret ingredient before returning to their respective kitchens.

The colorful dishes produced reflect that both chefs went out of their way to incorporate as much of the local produce as possible from the Nickel City Chef pantry provided by Wegmans. Interestingly, both chefs topped their dessert courses with vanilla yogurt ice cream, made from scratch on-site. I'm quite sure it was delicious, but this competition took place in August, and the ice cream didn't stand a chance.

The capabilities of White Cow Dairy's remarkable dairy products and our chefs were evident. All the dishes were tasty, but in the end, Jenkins' inspired lamb kibbeh and maple syrup-drizzled blueberry yogurt cake (page 27) won the hearts of the judges.

Nate Peracchny

CHALLENGING CHEF BRUCE WIESZALA'S

White Gazpacho

Servings: 6 | Total prep and cooking time: 30 minutes

INGREDIENTS

4 large cucumbers, peeled, seeded and diced

4 slices day-old baguette

3 tablespoons Marcona almonds

1 clove garlic

3/4 pound seedless green grapes, plus 8 sliced for garnish

3 tablespoons sherry vinegar

1/2 cup White Cow Dairy plain yogurt

3/4 cup extra virgin olive oil

Salt and pepper

DIRECTIONS

• Lightly toast the almonds in a small skillet over medium-low heat until golden. Transfer the almonds to a food processor. Add the garlic and pulse until the almonds are finely ground. Set aside.

• In a blender, add the cucumbers, grapes, yogurt, almond/garlic mixture, and sherry vinegar. Add salt and pepper to taste. Purée. Begin adding the bread in small pieces until fully incorporated. Add the olive oil in a steady stream until fully combined. Taste and reseason, if necessary.

• Transfer the gazpacho to a storage container and refrigerate for at least 6 hours.

PLATING

When ready to serve, ladle equal portions into four chilled bowls. Garnish each with a few sliced grapes and a drizzle of high-quality extra virgin olive oil.

Nancy J. Parisi

NICKEL CITY CHEF PAUL JENKINS'

Blueberry Cake
with Maple Syrup

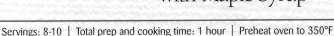

Servings: 8-10 | Total prep and cooking time: 1 hour | Preheat oven to 350°F

INGREDIENTS

1 cup sugar

2 teaspoons cinnamon

1/4 teaspoon nutmeg

2 tablespoons cold butter, cubed

1/2 cup unsalted butter

1 1/2 cups brown sugar

2 eggs

2 1/4 cups flour

1 teaspoon baking soda

1 cup White Cow Dairy plain yogurt

1 teaspoon pure vanilla extract

1/2 teaspoon lemon zest

2 cups blueberries

Warm New York maple syrup for serving

Vanilla ice cream

DIRECTIONS

• Butter and flour a 9 by 13-inch baking pan.

• Topping: In a small bowl combine sugar and cinnamon. Using a fork, blend chilled butter bits into sugar mixture until it forms large crumbs. Set aside.

• In a standing electric mixer or with a hand mixer, cream together butter and sugar. Add eggs and mix well. Add flour, baking soda, yogurt, vanilla, and zest. Mix on medium for 4 minutes. Pour batter into prepared pan and sprinkle top with blueberries. Lightly press them into batter, if needed. Top with crumble topping. Bake for 45 minutes. Cool on a rack.

PLATING

Plate individually using a rustic presentation. A simple piece of cake topped with a handful of fresh blueberries, some good-quality vanilla ice cream, and a drizzle of warm New York maple syrup.

28

CHALLENGING CHEF
Bruce Wieszala
of Verbena Grille

Mediterranean Tasting
• White Gazpacho
• Mussels in Broth
• Stuffed Eggplant Fritter

Butter-poached Lobster Tail
Handmade Tagliatelle, Black Truffle

Peach Bread Pudding
Housemade Vanilla Bean Yogurt Ice Cream

NICKEL CITY CHEF
Paul Jenkins
of Tempo

Cue Ball Squash
Corn and Quark Risotto

Lamb Kibbeh
Handmade Pita, Summer Vegetables

Blueberry Yogurt Cake
Maple Syrup, Housemade Vanilla Yogurt Ice Cream

SCORES FOR CHALLENGE 3

Challenging Chef Bruce Wieszala		Nickel City Chef Paul Jenkins	
Taste & Flavor	10	Taste & Flavor	10
Creativity	8	Creativity	11
Plating & Presentation	9	Plating & Presentation	11
Technical Execution	10	Technical Execution	9
Use of Secret Ingredient	11	Use of Secret Ingredient	10
Audience Vote	0	Audience Vote	1
Total	**48**		**52**

The Challenger:
Bruce Wieszala
Carmelo's
425 Center Street, Lewiston
carmelos-restaurant.com

Nate Peracciny

Bruce Wieszala is a Buffalo native who returned to the area after spending a decade in Atlanta. There, he worked in the kitchens of that city's best dining destinations, including Emeril's, the James Beard award-winning JOËL, Woodfire Grill, the five-star Mobile-rated Seeger's, and Restaurant Eugene. During his time down south he had the opportunity to compete on the Food Network's *Iron Chef America* as a sous to challenger Chef Linton Hopkins. He also appeared on the network's *Good Eats,* hosted by Alton Brown.

Since his return to Buffalo he has worked in several area restaurants, most notably as the executive chef at the former Verbena Grille. When Verbena shuttered, Chef Wieszala moved to Bistro Europa, a promising young restaurant dedicated to sourcing locally and making everything from scratch using wholesome ingredients.

Currently, Chef Wieszala is found in the kitchen of the award-winning Carmelo's in Lewiston, where his trademark charcuterie skills and passion for locally sourced foods are showcased beside the restaurant's chef/owner Carmelo Raimondi. Chef Wieszala continues to spread his love of butchery by teaching his methods and techniques at local culinary schools and in public forums.

> "He had the opportunity to compete on the Food Network's *Iron Chef America* as a sous chef."

CHALLENGE 4

Potatoes

FROM PROMISED LAND CSA

VS.

Nickel City Chef
Adam Goetz
Sample, Buffalo, NY

Challenging Chef
Kate Elliott
Juniper, Buffalo, NY

Oles Family Farm/ Promised Land CSA

Alden, New York   promisedlandcsa.com

The Oles family has been quietly and happily farming in Alden, New York since the late 1970s, providing outreach and interacting with the community through its produce stand and seasonal celebrations hosted at the farm. It is only in the last few years that they've entered the local food scene spotlight, and it has shined brightly. Potatoes from the Oles' Promised Land CSA were a brilliant choice as a Nickel City Chef secret ingredient, with the chefs' creations proving how deserving of attention the family, the farm, and the produce truly are.

Daniel Oles' father, Jack Oles, always dreamed of owning his own farm. In 1963, after nearly a decade of farming on rented land, he moved his family to Happy Meadows farm in Alden. Aspiring to take over the farm from his father, Daniel graduated from Cornell University in 1979 with a degree in Farm Business Management. He recalls learning the then-current approach to farming: bigger is better; plant only one or two cash crops over all your acreage to achieve the best results.

After college, Daniel married Jane, and they began working the farm alongside his family. Gradually, the couple took over the day-to-day operations of the farm with their four young children. Through continued communication with Cornell University and the agricultural community, Daniel and Jane slowly realized that the commodity farming practices they were using were not sustainable. In 1986, they began to implement more sustainable practices, and since the early 2000s, they have been farming organically.

Some of the current sustainable, organic practices in use at the Oles Family Farm include crop rotation, integrated pest management, cover crops, and the use of livestock as natural pest control and fertilizers. The family has noticed significant changes in their land and corresponding ecosystem since they ceased using herbicides and pesticides, including the return of helpful flora and fauna living positively in symbiosis.

After much research and discussion, the Oles family introduced Promised Land CSA in 2007, further promoting these sustainable practices. There were just eight members of the Community Supported Agriculture (CSA) initiative at the start of the inaugural season, but forty by its end. Membership has doubled each season since then, and topped 250 in 2011.

Putting their beliefs into practice and staying at the forefront of agricultural trends has unintentionally positioned the Oles family as one of the go-to sources for other farmers seeking advice, consumers seeking information, and members of the restaurant industry seeking delicious, diverse, organically grown food. In fact, each week, the Oles Family Farm's relationships in the industry result in delivery of fresh produce from the farm directly to the back door of nearly a dozen local restaurant kitchens.

The family grows a remarkable variety of produce on its farm, made possible by both its careful and respectful handling of the soil and the demand of its dedicated CSA and restaurant clients. Blueberries, broccoli, greens, strawberries, Brussels sprouts, squash, and fresh herbs are just a few of the forty or more items grown each year.

The farm also now features several greenhouses that extend the growing season and allow the Oles to provide food to restaurant customers nearly year-round. And they continue to reach out to consumers and other farmers to encourage sustainable growing practices and educate them about the importance of buying local food. The Oles family has hosted several farm tours for chefs, countless children's farm experiences, and even fine dining events right on the farm.

When approached about the possibility of using potatoes as a Nickel City Chef secret ingredient, Daniel Oles offered not one variety, but five. The farm's commitment to providing a varied, flavorful, and healthy diet of fruits and vegetables to its customers makes each CSA share and each restaurant delivery an inspiring experience for those who love to cook...and eat.

Many find the Oles' potatoes to be sweeter than most. The Oles believe this exceptional flavor is imparted by the soil on their Erie County farm.

kc kratt

The final competition of the first season took place in September 2009, and like the previous three shows that summer, sold out quickly. Nickel City Chef Adam Goetz of Sample and challenger Kate Elliott of the newly opened Juniper seemed equally nervous and excited about the competition. They also both exhibited good sportsmanship, and while I don't doubt for a second that each wanted to win, they worked to keep the competition light by focusing on the fun inherent in the challenge of cooking before a live audience.

When it opened in late 2007, Sample made quite a splash among area restaurant critics with its original concept of serving food in hors d'oeuvres-sized portions accompanied by remarkable from-scratch cocktails. Juniper was also new on the scene and, like Sample, had received good reviews early on. The Elmwood Village eatery featured a colorful interior and an inventive menu that attracted a steady stream of customers from the day it opened. We were pleased to offer Chef Elliott and her sous chef, Roo Buckley, a chance to expose their unique culinary approach to an audience of local foodies.

The chefs were able to choose from among five delicious varieties of potatoes: Rose Gold, Yukon Gold, Adirondack Red, Adirondack Blue, and French Fingerling. This provided them with ample opportunity to use the potatoes' array of colors and textures to their advantage, since each of the varieties has its own unique characteristics. Anyone who has tasted a potato from the Oles' farm can confirm that their potatoes are especially sweet and flavorful due in part, to the composition of the soil in which they are grown.

"Chef Elliott made use of the stunning Adirondack Blue potatoes, which gave her soup a violet hue."

During the competition, the two chefs prepared only one similar dish: vichyssoise. Chef Elliott made use of the stunning Adirondack Blue potatoes, which gave her soup a violet hue. She then dressed it up with a lobster tail and tarragon-infused oil. It was much thicker than most vichyssoise recipes, but in the end it managed to trump Goetz's version, which may have been too cute for its own good. His vichyssoise was glossy and velvety, made with white potatoes so that it could act as "milk" to his tiny fried-potato gnocchi, which were shaped like Cheerios. Unfortunately, while the idea behind this dish was to showcase Buffalo's love of its waterfront Cheerios factory and the creative reinvention of two classic potato dishes, this clever concept seemed lost on the judges.

All of the courses exhibited interesting use of the beautiful, multihued potatoes. They were crafted into a risotto-style base for Chef Elliott's tender rabbit dish and puréed into breathtakingly beautiful vinaigrettes served with Chef Goetz's potato medallion, which he flavored to taste like a fine cut of beef. It was a fabulous afternoon filled with inventive food and a congenial atmosphere fostered by the positive and affable attitude of both chefs and their fans. Little did we know then that Nickel City Chef would be such a hit that another eight shows would be scheduled to begin just a few short months later.

Nickel City Chef Adam Goetz carefully plates his first course of vichyssoise "milk" and potato gnocchi "Cheerios."

LEl Photography

Rabbit Loin
with Risotto and Maple Harissa

Servings: 8 | Total prep and cooking time: 1 hour | Preheat oven to 400°F

INGREDIENTS

8 4-6 ounce rabbit loins
16 slices Serrano ham
Lemon basil leaves
Salt and pepper

5 Rose Gold potatoes
5 Yukon Gold potatoes
2 cups Muenster cheese, shredded
1/4 cup chervil, fresh
1 shallot, diced
2 cups heavy cream
3 tablespoons butter
Salt and pepper

3/4 cup extra virgin olive oil
1/4 cup New York maple syrup
1 cup chili powder
1 teaspoon ground caraway
1 teaspoon ground cardamom
1 tablespoon ground coriander
1 tablespoon kosher salt
2 cloves garlic, minced

DIRECTIONS

Rabbit Loin

• Separate the loins, trimming any sinew. Pat dry with a paper towel and season with salt and pepper. On a cutting board, lay out, vertically and slightly overlapping, two slices of ham for each loin as though you were going to wrap a gift. At the bottom of the ham–the part closest to you on the cutting board–place a row of fresh basil. Lay a loin on top and roll it up in the ham. Wrap each package tightly in plastic wrap and refrigerate for at least 30 minutes.

• When ready to serve, remove the wrapped loins from the refrigerator. Heat an ovenproof sauté pan on the stove top. Remove the plastic wrap from each loin and place the loins in the pan, searing each side for a minute to attain color and a little crispness. Move the pan to the oven and cook for 15 minutes.

Potato Risotto

• Peel potatoes and dice. The smaller and more even the dice, the better the result. Melt the butter in a pan at least three inches deep.

• Add the shallot, cooking until translucent. Over medium heat, add the potatoes, stirring constantly and allowing them to brown slightly.

• Reduce the heat to low and allow a few minutes for the temperature of the pan to decrease. Add enough heavy cream to barely cover the potatoes. Reduce liquid by half, stirring the entire time to prevent scorching. Check for doneness.

• Remove from heat and incorporate the cheese, fresh chervil, and salt and pepper to taste.

Maple Harissa Sauce

• Heat a small saucepan. Add all the ingredients and infuse the flavors by keeping the pan over a low flame for 45 minutes. Strain through a fine-mesh sieve. Reserve.

PLATING

Place "risotto" in the center of a pasta bowl or deep plate. Place loin on top and drizzle sparingly with Maple Harissa. For an extra special garnish, try bruléeing fresh figs with a little brown sugar, or deep frying a fine julienne of fresh ginger.

NICKEL CITY CHEF ADAM GOETZ'S
Batatada Cake
with Whipped Ricotta, Blueberry Port Reduction, and Mint Oil

Servings: 4 | Total prep and cooking time: 1 hour | Preheat oven to 350°F

INGREDIENTS

1 2/3 cups warm mashed potatoes (not instant)
1/4 cup heavy cream
1/4 cup evaporated milk
3/4 cup room temperature unsalted butter
1 egg
3 egg yolks
1 cup sugar
1/2 cup all-purpose flour
1/2 teaspoon baking powder
Nonstick pan spray

DIRECTIONS

Batatada Cake

• Place sugar and eggs in a stand mixer with the paddle attachment. Mix on medium speed. Add butter and combine. Add potatoes, cream, and milk. Mix. Add baking powder and flour and mix briefly until combined.

• Spray individual cake or tart pans and add batter. Place in the oven and bake until a toothpick comes out clean, about 30 minutes. Remove from oven and allow to cool. Remove from pans.

Note: it is easier to remove the cakes when they are still slightly warm. After they have cooled completely, slice them once horizontally to make layers.

---

2 cups whole milk ricotta, drained thoroughly
1 cup heavy cream

Whipped Ricotta

• Place ricotta in a food processor with the blade attachment and pulse a few times to break up the cheese. Turn on the processor, slowly adding the heavy cream. Depending on how dry the ricotta is, it may take more or less cream. Combine until the result is similar to a thick icing.

---

2 cups ruby port
2 cups fresh blueberries
1/4 cup sugar

Blueberry Port Reduction

• Put all ingredients in a sauce pan and bring to a boil over medium heat. Reduce the port on simmer until a thick a sauce forms. It should be mostly blueberries with a little thick liquid. Be careful when cooking the port as it has a tendency to flame up. If it does, extinguish flames by placing a lid on the pot temporarily. Remove from heat and allow to cool.

---

4 cups mint leaves
4 cups water
2 cups sugar
3/4 cup canola oil

Mint Oil

• Prepare a small ice-water bath. Set aside. Bring the water and sugar to a boil in a sauce pan. Place the mint leaves in the boiling water and sugar mixture and cook for 45 seconds. Remove the leaves to the water bath to cool. Place mint and oil in a blender, combining until the leaves are puréed. Strain through a fine-mesh strainer.

PLATING

Lay one layer of the cake on a plate. Spread a generous amount of the whipped ricotta on top. Cover with another layer of cake. Make as many layers as you wish–but at least two. On the final layer, place a dollop of the ricotta mixture, and spoon the cooled blueberries and their sauce on top. Finish by drizzling with a modest amount of sweet mint oil. You may also wish to garnish with a little powdered sugar.

34

CHALLENGING CHEF
Kate Elliott
of Juniper

Blue Potato Vichyssoise
Maple-poached Lobster, Tarragon Oil

Rabbit Loin, Lemon Basil and Serrano Ham, Potato Risotto, Maple Harissa, Bruléed Figs

Sweet Potato and Rose Gold Flan
Rosemary Mousse, Walnut Cigar

NICKEL CITY CHEF
Adam Goetz
of Sample

Breakfast & Lunch Tasting:
• Gnocchi "Cheerios" with Vichyssoise Milk
• Housemade Pork Potato Sausage with Peppers and Onions

"Beef Medallion" of Potato
Beef Jus, Mashed Potato Foam, Purple Potato Vinaigrette

Layered Potato Batatada Cake
Whipped Ricotta, Blueberry Port Sauce, and Mint Oil

SCORES FOR CHALLENGE 4

	Challenging Chef Kate Elliot		Nickel City Chef Adam Goetz
Taste & Flavor	12	Taste & Flavor	11
Creativity	11	Creativity	10
Plating & Presentation	10	Plating & Presentation	9
Technical Execution	12	Technical Execution	9
Use of Secret Ingredient	11	Use of Secret Ingredient	10
Audience Vote	0	Audience Vote	1
Total	**56**		**50**

The Challenger:
Chef Kate Elliott

Merge
439 Delaware Avenue, Buffalo, New York
mergebuffalo.com

Kate Elliott developed her unique cooking style not through formal culinary training, but rather by working her way through Buffalo's kitchens for more than fifteen years. In 2009 she opened Juniper, an exciting and innovative restaurant that was well received by the community and critics alike.

Today, she can be found in the role of executive chef at the city's most popular health-conscious restaurant, Merge. There, her focus on fresh, local food matches perfectly with the restaurant's ethos of organic, free-range, and healthful. Chef Elliott masterfully assembles vegan and vegetarian ingredients into delicious takes on classic offerings such as pot roast and fettuccine Alfredo.

Merge has become a gathering place for thinkers, grassroots activists, and those who wish to build a new Buffalo. Elliott's food philosophy melds ideally with this lofty attitude, since it celebrates creativity, health, and the warmth and communal atmosphere of gathering around the table to break bread with friends.

> **Chef Elliott masterfully assembles vegan and vegetarian ingredients into delicious takes on classic offerings.**

CHALLENGE 5

Ricotta Cheese

FROM SORRENTO®

 VS.

Nickel City Chef
Adam Goetz
Sample, Buffalo, NY

Challenging Chef
Ross Warhol
Athenaeum Hotel,
Chautauqua, NY

Sorrento® Cheese

Buffalo, New York sorrentocheese.com

Western New York boasts a large Italian population—and a hearty appetite for Italian food. With ricotta cheese such an integral component of classic Italian desserts such as cannoli and cassata cake, as well as savory dishes like ravioli, manicotti, and lasagna, it makes sense that a business specializing in the production of ricotta cheese would have deep roots in the region. And who knows ricotta better than Sorrento®? As a Nickel City Chef secret ingredient, Sorrento's ricotta cheese allowed the chefs to consider Buffalo's past, while creating something thrillingly new in the present.

Sorrento® has been based in Buffalo since 1947, when cheese-maker Louis Russo, an immigrant from Sorrento, Italy, began producing ricotta cheese from an age-old family recipe. The business was a local hit. Sorrento® trucks could be found delivering cheese products to Italian restaurants and corner grocery stores all over town. In fact, the company became so successful that in 1986 it was able to purchase Precious Cheese, expanding to become a national brand.

In the mid-1990s, Sorrento® became part of Groupe Lactalis, the largest producer of cheese in the world. Now known as Lactalis Retail Dairy, this local company, and New York City-based Lactalis Deli, form the Lactalis American Group.

Sorrento's bustling South Buffalo headquarters is one of the largest ricotta manufacturers in the world. But this is not the only high-quality product coming out of the plant; provolone, mozzarella, and whey-powder are produced there as well. A second plant in Nampa, Idaho, produces Sorrento's fresh mozzarella, mascarpone, and snacking cheeses.

Not only are Sorrento's cheeses sold in supermarkets all over the country, but the company also has a firm foothold in the foodservice industry and shows continued growth, having acquired both Rondele and Mozzarella Fresca in recent years. This rapid expansion means that the Sorrento® of today is much larger than the humble company of 1947, but the whole milk ricotta recipe is generations old. Interestingly, ricotta is not technically a cheese at all, since it is made from whey, a by-product of

the process of turning milk into cheeses like provolone and mozzarella. Its origins date back centuries. The name means "re-cooked" in Italian, referring to the process by which the cheese is made.

Sorrento® continues to maintain a focus on freshness and quality, and this is evident in the awards they have received for Sorrento® Whole Milk Ricotta Cheese, including the American Cheese Society Silver Medal (2009), the World Dairy Expo Silver Medal (2009), and the Los Angeles International Dairy Competition Gold Medal (2009).

As the secret ingredient of the fifth Nickel City Chef challenge, Sorrento's ricotta cheese sparked some of the finest, most carefully crafted dishes in the series. This amazingly versatile ingredient was used in a mind-boggling number of applications by both chefs.

The edible and economic benefits of having a nationally acclaimed soft cheese producer in our own backyard are obvious—Sorrento® sponsors the second-largest Italian Festival in the U.S. in North Buffalo every July, for example—but the edible benefits are clear, too, on dinner tables throughout Western New York.

Sorrento® has been making quality cheese in South Buffalo since 1947, including whole milk ricotta, the secret ingredient in Challenge 5.

36

W̱ere food quality the only measure, Challenge: Ricotta would be, without a doubt, the best event of the three-season series. Nickel City Chef Adam Goetz of Sample and challenger Chef Ross Warhol of Chautauqua Institution's Athenaeum Hotel were well matched, and every dish prepared was practically a work of art. Both competitors clearly understood the importance of showcasing the secret ingredient, and the audience and our judges left in a bit of a stupor, having seen some of the most inventive and beautiful dishes imaginable.

The ricotta challenge was especially interesting because ricotta cheese is so versatile, useable in both sweet and savory applications. As a protein, it can play a major role in a dish, but as a soft cheese it can easily be incorporated into a sauce or other accompaniment. Using a product with such flexibility might seem easy, but it takes a talented hand to ensure that ricotta's gentle flavor is not lost. Both chefs did a superb job, and set a high standard for how the best of the best in Western New York looks and tastes.

Chef Goetz amazed the judges with his first course, a multi-component "tasting" featuring ricotta prepared in five different ways. In the end, Goetz's three-course menu included more than thirty different elements, meaning that he had less than two minutes to create each one within the Nickel City Chef restrictive sixty-minute time limit. No wonder his kitchen required the use of six blenders!

"...the audience and our judges left in a bit of a stupor, having seen some of the most inventive and beautiful dishes imaginable."

Chef Warhol may be young, but he is also skilled and talented. His kitchen remained remarkably clean and well organized throughout the battle, the sign of a truly disciplined chef. At his side was his mentor, Daniel Johenghen, one of Buffalo's top chefs and owner of the respected Hamburg, New York restaurant, Daniel's.

Although Chef Warhol trained under Johenghen, it was clear the menu was all his own. His penchant for modern cooking (called molecular gastronomy by some) played into each dish, most notably his dessert. To remain within the time limitations, Warhol used a special method to bake his almond cake in a microwave oven. It emerged surprisingly light and flavorful, with good texture. His Lemon Ricotta Ice Cream (page 38) was divine, but the addition of poached plums, chocolate hazelnut powder, and pliable chocolate ganache put this offering at the top of the heap as one of the best desserts ever created in the Nickel City Chef kitchens.

One of this competition's judges was John Bourdage, a food and beverage consultant who writes about wine for various publications. After the show he spoke on camera: "Both chefs were incredible....We've been tagged as the beef-on-'weck city, but there's so much more. This event really showcases that."

Nickel City Chef Adam Goetz served a ricotta and quail egg ravioli as part of his five-part first course which he named "Ricotta Tasting."

Nate Peracciny

CHALLENGE 5: RICOTTA CHEESE FROM SORRENTO®

CHEF ROSS WARHOL'S

Lemon Ricotta Ice Cream

with Almond Cake, Poached Plum, Chocolate Ganache, and Hazelnut Powder

Servings: 6-8 | Total prep and cooking time: 2 hours | Preheat oven to 375°F

INGREDIENTS

1 cup water
1 cup sugar
3 tablespoons fresh lemon juice
2 1/2 cups whole milk ricotta cheese
2 teaspoons New York honey
1/2 teaspoon salt

DIRECTIONS

Ice Cream

• Combine the sugar and water in a saucepan over medium heat. Bring to a boil. Remove from heat, transfer to a bowl, and add the lemon juice. Refrigerate for 20 minutes. In a blender combine the ricotta, honey, and salt. Process until smooth. Slowly drizzle the chilled lemon syrup into the blender while it is running on low. Process mixture in an ice cream machine according to the manufacturer's directions. Hold in freezer until ready to plate.

3/4 + 1/8 cup almond paste
3/4 cup + 2 tablespoons unsalted butter
Scant 1 cup sugar
6 eggs
3/4 cup cake flour

Almond Cake

• Using a stand mixer, cream the almond paste, butter, and sugar with the paddle attachment on medium speed until light and fluffy, approximately 10 minutes. Whisk the eggs in a separate bowl. Add to the mixer in two or three portions, scraping down the side of the bowl after each addition. Once the eggs are fully incorporated, add the flour and mix on low speed until the batter becomes smooth. Line a half sheet tray (13 1/2 x 17 1/2 inches) with parchment and spread the batter evenly. Bake for 20 to 25 minutes. Remove from oven and cool on a rack.

---

1 3/4 cups red wine, preferably Beaujolais
1/2 cup sugar
1/2 vanilla bean, split and scraped
2 tea bags, Earl Gray
4 fresh plums, halved and pitted

Poached Plums

• In a saucepan over medium heat, combine wine, sugar, and vanilla. Bring to a boil. Remove from heat and add the tea bags. Steep for 10 minutes. Discard the tea bags. Add the plums to the syrup and place over low heat. Bring to a low simmer and poach for 10 minutes. Remove from heat and set aside until plating.

Scant 1/2 cup chocolate hazelnut spread (60%)
3 tablespoons + 1/2 teaspoon maltodextrin tapioca* (40%)

This is a special order ingredient available through various online culinary suppliers.

Chocolate Hazelnut Powder

• Chill the bowl, blade, and lid of the food processor for 20 minutes. Pour the maltodextrin into the food processor. Add the chocolate hazelnut. Pulse to combine. Process until the chocolate hazelnut is fully absorbed by the maltodextrin. Pass the powder through a fine strainer and reserve in an airtight container.

1 1/2 cups dark chocolate (72% cacao), chopped

1 cup cream

Chocolate Ganache

• Heat cream in a sauce pan over medium-high heat just until it comes to a boil. Place the chocolate in a mixing bowl. Pour the hot cream over the chocolate and allow to stand for 5 minutes. Whisk the ganache until smooth. Pour into a tray or dish of the desired thickness and cool in the refrigerator. Cut ganache into pieces and reserve for plating.

PLATING With so many components, it is easy to make this dish look messy. Less is more when it comes to quantity. Consider varying the shape of things, such as cutting the cake into rounds and serving the ganache as a rectangle and the ice cream in a quenelle. This variety will add visual beauty to your plate, as will a sprinkle of edible flower petals or a few slices of fresh red berry.

Nancy J. Parisi

NICKEL CITY CHEF ADAM GOETZ'S
Roasted Monkfish
with Ricotta Gnocchi and Ricotta Foam

Servings: 4 | Total prep and cooking time: 1 hour | Preheat oven to 350°F

INGREDIENTS

1 cup whole milk ricotta cheese, strained

2 eggs

1/2 cup grated Parmesan-Reggiano

1 teaspoon kosher salt

1 teaspoon white pepper

1 cup all-purpose flour

Nonstick pan spray

DIRECTIONS

Ricotta Gnocchi

- Place the cheese, eggs, salt, and pepper in a mixing bowl and combine. Add the Parmesan and mix well. Slowly incorporate the flour, combining until a dough starts to form. Depending on how dry the ricotta is, you may need more or less flour. The dough should be the consistency of children's play dough. Remove the dough from the bowl and cover with a cloth. Flour a cutting board and roll out long logs of dough about the thickness of your index finger. Cut the logs into gnocchi, about 1/2" thick. Reserve on a floured baking sheet or plate.

- Bring a large pot of salted water to boil over medium-high heat. Place the gnocchi in the pot and cook until they float. Remove gnocchi from water and reserve on a baking sheet sprayed with a little nonstick pan spray.

- When ready to serve, sauté the gnocchi in hot butter. Season with salt and pepper.

1 monkfish loin, cleaned

1 lemon, zested

1 tablespoon crushed red pepper flakes

1/4 cup flat leaf Italian parsley, chopped

2 tablespoons fresh thyme leaves

Canola oil for cooking

Roasted Monkfish

- On a plate or wax paper, combine the lemon zest, parsley, and thyme. Roll the monkfish, covering thoroughly and evenly. Cover with plastic wrap (or wrap loosely in the wax paper) and refrigerate for 20 minutes.

- Remove the loin from the refrigerator and uncover. Sprinkle the loin on all sides with kosher salt. Heat a nonstick sauté pan on high. Add 2 to 4 tablespoons of oil. Sear the loin quickly. Once the outside is seared and has a little color, remove and place on a baking sheet. Roast in the oven for 10 to 15 minutes until the flesh is firm to the touch. Remove from heat and let rest for 5 minutes. Slice into medallions and serve with sauce and gnocchi.

1/2 yellow onion, sliced

5 cloves garlic, crushed

2 cups heavy cream

5 sprigs parsley

5 sprigs thyme

1/2 cup whole milk ricotta cheese

Ricotta Foam Sauce

- Place a saucepan over low heat. Add onion, garlic, cream, parsley, and thyme. Let simmer for 15 minutes. Strain the mixture, reserving the flavored cream. Place the ricotta in a blender and add half the cream mixture. Blend until smooth. Whisk in the remaining cream and add salt and pepper to taste. Return the mixture to the sauce pan and keep warm until ready to serve. Use a thermal whip to make this sauce into a foam. If you do not have a thermal whip, you can use an immersion blender to froth the sauce, scooping up the bubbles with a spoon.

PLATING Place the sautéed gnocchi in a rectangular shape in the middle of the plate. Add the medallions of monkfish on top of the gnocchi. Place the ricotta foam around the fish. This dish is even better when served with shiitake mushrooms that have been crisped in butter.

CHALLENGE 5: RICOTTA CHEESE FROM SORRENTO®

40

CHALLENGING CHEF
Ross Warhol
of the Athenaeum Hotel

Warm Ricotta Plaque
Shaved Vegetable Salad, Chorizo
Vinaigrette, Tomato Ricotta Cornet

Honey-glazed Duck Breast
Ricotta Scallion Pancakes, Succotash,
Ricotta Foam

Lemon Ricotta Ice Cream
Almond Cake, Poached Plum,
Chocolate Ganache, Chocolate
Hazelnut Powder

NICKEL CITY CHEF
Adam Goetz
of Sample

Ricotta Tasting:
• Olive Salad
• Roasted Tomato with Basil
• Lemon Ricotta Garlic Air
• Quail Egg Ravioli
• Ricotta Tarragon Gougère

Roasted Monkfish
Ricotta Gnocchi, Crispy
Shiitake, Ricotta Foam, Fennel
Frond Salad, Ricotta Vinaigrette

"Cannoli"
Espresso Ricotta Filling,
Cinnamon Chocolate Sauce,
Pomegranate Foam

CHALLENGE 5: RICOTTA CHEESE FROM SORRENTO®

	Challenging Chef Ross Warhol		Nickel City Chef Adam Goetz
Taste & Flavor	10	Taste & Flavor	12
Creativity	11	Creativity	11
Plating & Presentation	11	Plating & Presentation	11
Technical Execution	12	Technical Execution	12
Use of Secret Ingredient	11	Use of Secret Ingredient	12
Audience Vote	1	Audience Vote	0
Total	**56**		**58**

The Challenger:
Chef Ross Warhol
Athenaeum Hotel
Chautauqua Institution, Chautauqua, New York
athenaeum-hotel.com

Chef Warhol began his cooking career locally in the kitchen of Hamburg's esteemed Daniel's, under the watchful eye of well-respected chef Daniel Johengen. He then spent some time working in the kitchen of La Fleur, a AAA Four Diamond-rated restaurant in Mayville, New York, best known for its French seasonal cuisine.

Warhol next enrolled in the Culinary Institute of America in Hyde Park, New York, graduating from the Culinary Institute of America at Greystone in Napa Valley, California. While in Napa he worked at Wine Spectator Restaurant, and then interned at a number of world-renowned restaurants, including Napa's Ubuntu and the French Laundry, Chicago's Alinea, and, most notably, Catalonia, Spain's elBulli, long considered the world's best restaurant.

Since his return to the Buffalo area, he has taken on the seasonal role of executive chef at the Athenaeum, located inside the gates of the Chautauqua Institution. Warhol's passion for local ingredients and seasonal produce has led him to plant organic gardens in both Napa and Chautauqua. His commitment to these principles and his passion for new, modern cooking techniques have already earned him a reputation for creating exciting and flavorful cuisine.

> **His passion for local ingredients and seasonal produce has led him to plant organic gardens in both Napa and Chautauqua.**

CHALLENGE 6

Shiitake Mushrooms

FROM GREEN HERON GROWERS

 VS.

Nickel City Chef
JJ Richert
Torches, Buffalo, NY

Challenging Chef
Carmelo Raimondi
Carmelo's, Lewiston, NY

Green Heron Growers

Panama, New York   greenherongrowers.com

Each summer, thousands of music fans descend on Steve and Julie Rockcastle's beautiful farm in Chautauqua County, but their visit has nothing to do with food. For nearly two decades, the famous and wildly popular Great Blue Heron Music Festival has transformed the pastures that make up Green Heron Growers into campgrounds and music stages. But it is what happens on the Rockcastle property during the rest of the year that is of interest to foodies.

In recent years the couple has put its grassy fields and wooded acres to excellent use raising grass-fed cows, pasture-raised chickens, organic produce, and shiitake mushrooms. In the farm's natural hemlock grove, hundreds of three-foot oak, sugar maple, and beech logs are host to various stages of shiitake growth. These mighty mushrooms were a unique choice as a Nickel City Chef secret ingredient.

Shiitake are native to East Asia and have existed since prehistoric times. They have been cultivated for more than a thousand years and are prized for their smoky, meaty texture. At Green Heron Growers, the Rockcastles drill holes in the oak, sugar maple, and beech logs, filling them with mycelium. They then seal the holes with wax and wait for as long as eighteen months for shiitake to appear. Along the way a good deal of rotation, soaking, and pest management is required, but it is well worth the time and effort.

In 2010, the Rockcastles sold more than 650 pounds of shiitake mushrooms, along with a few value-added products, including their delicious Shiitake Hazelnut Paté. These were sold through an on-farm store, to everyday shoppers at a few local farmers' markets, and directly to chefs, as well.

A certified organic farm, Green Heron is often the site used for field courses offered by the New York chapter of the National Organic Farming Organization to teach other farmers how to grow mushrooms. And as the competitors in Nickel City Chef's sixth battle learned after being provided with large quantities of high-quality dried and fresh shiitake mushrooms, this is one versatile fungus.

Steve and Julie Rockcastle grow shiitake and produce on their farm in addition to raising fresh beef and chicken.

Green Heron Growers has been producing food for a relatively short time compared to many of Western New York's second- and third-generation farms. But in that time, the Rockcastles have developed a dedicated following by producing unique and especially delicious ingredients that speak to chefs and food lovers alike. Truly delicious Red Devon grass-fed beef and pasture-raised chickens are just two of the things they do better than most. Shiitake mushrooms are another.

Prior to their decision to raise mushrooms in their hemlock grove, no other farm in Western New York was raising mushrooms for either wholesale or retail sale, despite the fact that many factors make Western New York ideal for growing mushrooms. Perhaps other farmers will take note and many types of locally-raised mushrooms will be available someday soon.

"Chef Richert's use of a pressure cooker to turn chicken feet into a garnish for his dish proved to the audience and to skeptical host Bert Gambini how careful handling can turn even the least-appealing cut of meat into a delicious sweet-and-spicy flavor explosion."

One of the benefits of growing shiitake is that they can be dried, and dried shiitake were at the heart of this challenge. Both of the competing chefs, Nickel City Chef JJ Richert of Torches and Chef Carmelo Raimondi of Carmelo's, work with mushrooms in their restaurants, but shiitake can be mild; dried, they are even more delicate. Bringing their smoky and earthy flavor to the forefront in each dish was a challenge. Interestingly, both chefs chose to powder them for use as part of a dry rub for meat, an application that worked well.

Two of the best dishes were offered in the first course. Chef Richert's use of a pressure cooker to turn chicken feet into a garnish for his dish proved to the audience and to skeptical host Bert Gambini how careful handling can turn even the least-appealing cut of meat into a delicious sweet-and-spicy flavor explosion.

The judges were puzzled by Raimondi's sweet and savory dessert offering, a play on traditional cappuccino with notes of brandy, shiitake, lemon, and honey. Elements of it were very good, but it was hard to wrap one's mind around the marriage of such diverse flavors.

In the end, Richert beat Raimondi by only a single point. While the judges felt that Raimondi's food had a preferable flavor profile overall, in this challenge, Richert's creativity and good judgment in terms of plating and presentation prevailed.

Always a showman, Nickel City Chef Richert thrives under the pressure found in a competitive setting.

LEI Photography

Shiitake-dusted Pork Tenderloin
with Housemade Sausage

Servings: 4 | Total prep and cooking time: 1 hour | Preheat oven to 350°F

INGREDIENTS

2 pounds ground pork sausage

1 pork tenderloin (silver skin removed)

4 tablespoons dried shiitake mushroom powder
(use a spice grinder to grind dry mushrooms)

1 pound fresh shiitake mushrooms

1 pint cherry tomatoes

1 sprig fresh rosemary, leaves finely chopped

10 fresh sage leaves, finely chopped

10 fresh basil leaves, chopped

4 cloves garlic: 2 finely chopped, 2 thinly sliced

1/2 cup extra virgin olive oil

Salt and pepper

1 tablespoon anchovy paste

1 tablespoon balsamic vinegar

DIRECTIONS

Pork Tenderloins

• Place a 12 by 24-inch piece of plastic wrap on a large cutting board. Spread the raw ground sausage in a rectangle (aim for about 1/4" thickness) on the plastic wrap. Pat the tenderloin dry with paper towels. Season it on all sides with salt and pepper. Coat it thoroughly with shiitake mushroom powder. Place the tenderloin in the center of the sausage. Roll up the plastic wrap, covering the tenderloin with the sausage. Press firmly into place. Carefully remove just the plastic, using your hand to press the sausage around the tenderloin so that no tenderloin is exposed. Place the pork on a foil-lined sheet pan and cook until a thermometer gives an internal reading of 155°F. Allow to rest at room temperature 10 minutes before slicing and serving.

Roasted Shiitake Mushrooms

• In a small bowl, combine 1/4 cup of olive oil and the sage, rosemary, and chopped garlic. Whisk to blend.

• Place the mushrooms and tomatoes in a small roasting pan or casserole dish, covering with the herbed oil mixture. Season the mushrooms and tomatoes with salt and pepper and roast uncovered for 20 minutes. This step can be completed while the tenderloin roasts. When done, place the roasted vegetables in a mixing bowl, reserving the juices.

• In a separate bowl, combine the sliced garlic, anchovy paste, basil, balsamic vinegar, salt, and pepper. Gently whisk in 3 tablespoons of the olive oil and pour the mixture over the roasted mushrooms and tomatoes. Set aside.

PLATING

Arrange the mushroom mixture in the center of four warmed plates. Slice the pork into four even pieces and place them on the roasted vegetables. Drizzle with the reserved roasted vegetable liquid.

Chef's notes

You can put the pork and the mushrooms in the oven at the same time. This dish is fabulous when served with roasted rosemary potatoes that have been lightly tossed in truffle oil.

44

Nancy J. Parisi

NICKEL CITY CHEF JJ RICHERT'S
Shiitake Broth
with Asian Accoutrements

Servings: 8 | Total prep and cooking time: 3 hours

INGREDIENTS

2 tablespoons fresh chopped ginger

2 tablespoons chopped garlic

2 tablespoons chopped green onion

4 cups shiitake mushrooms

1/2 gallon water

4 cups sake rice wine

1/4 cup soy sauce

1/2 cup chopped leek

1/2 cup chopped carrot

1/2 cup chopped celery

8 chicken feet

Salt

DIRECTIONS

• In a large stock pot combine the ginger, garlic, onion, and sesame oil. Sauté until aromatic. Add the shiitake mushrooms, water, sake, soy, leek, carrot, celery, and chicken feet. Bring to a boil over medium-high heat. Simmer for two and a half hours. Strain the concentrated broth into a smaller pot and simmer on low heat. Discard strained ingredients.

GARNISH OPTIONS

Fresh bean sprouts

Pork dumplings

Sliced green onion

Quail eggs

Sweet chili sauce

Cooked crab meat

Sesame seeds

Sliced shiitake mushrooms

PLATING

Place your choice of garnishes in serving bowls, for example: one raw quail egg, a handful of bean sprouts, some finely chopped green onion, a cooked pork dumpling, cooked crab meat, sesame seeds, and sliced shiitake mushrooms. Add stock and a drizzle of sweet chili sauce. You can serve this nicely at a dinner party by taking the broth to the table separately, adding it, piping hot, from a teapot or coffee warmer tableside.

CHALLENGE 6: SHIITAKE MUSHROOMS FROM GREEN HERON GROWERS

CHALLENGING CHEF
Carmelo Raimondi
of Carmelo's

Ricotta Gnocchi
Shiitake, Pancetta, Red Chard, Sage
Brown Butter

Shiitake-dusted Pork Tenderloin
Housemade Sausage, Warmed
Shiitake and Tomato Salad

"Shiitake-cino"
Brandy Cream, Gruyère Shiitake
Beignet, Lemon Honey

NICKEL CITY CHEF
JJ Richert
of Torches

Shiitake Broth
Fresh Quail Egg, Pork Dumpling,
Crab, Chicken Foot, Enoki
Mushroom, Mustard Microgreens

Shiitake Roulade
Tasso Ham, Dried Shiitake,
Marsala Cream

Shiitake Smoked Surf & Turf
Aged Prime Rib Eye Rubbed
with Coffee, Cocoa, and Shiitake
Powder, Shiitake Flour-coated
Calamari, Shiitake-dusted
Gnocchi

SCORES FOR CHALLENGE 6

	Challenging Chef Carmelo Raimondi		Nickel City Chef JJ Richert
Taste & Flavor	12	Taste & Flavor	10
Creativity	9	Creativity	11
Plating & Presentation	9	Plating & Presentation	11
Technical Execution	11	Technical Execution	10
Use of Secret Ingredient	10	Use of Secret Ingredient	11
Audience Vote	1	Audience Vote	0
Total	**52**		**53**

The Challenger:
Carmelo Raimondi
Carmelo's
425 Center Street, Lewiston
carmelos-restaurant.com

Carmelo Raimondi is the second-generation chef/owner of Carmelo's in Lewiston. Recognized for its refined and contemporary take on classic Italian preparations, Carmelo's has been in business for more than thirty years. It might come as a surprise, then, that Chef Raimondi has no formal training. He learned most of his skills at the side of his father, who passed away while his son was still in college.

Returning home to run the family business, Raimondi sought inspiration and found it in the fields of Niagara County's many farms. His dedication to local farmers and food artisans is evident in the freshness and quality of his constantly evolving seasonal menu. His desire to leave the world a better place for his children has driven him to develop many efficiencies and conservation methods, making Carmelo's a leader in Western New York's growing green restaurant movement. Chef Raimondi lives in the Village of Lewiston with his wife and young children.

> His desire to leave the world a better place for his children has driven him to develop many efficiencies and conservation methods.

46

CHALLENGE 7

Concord Grape Concentrate

FROM GRAPE GROWERS' COOPERATIVE

 VS.

Nickel City Chef
Paul Jenkins
Tempo, Buffalo, NY

Challenging Chef
Keith Dulak
Trattoria Aroma, Buffalo, NY

Growers' Cooperative Grape Juice Company

Westfield, New York   concordgrapejuice.com

The Lake Erie grape region of Chautauqua County is where it's at when it comes to Concord grapes. Sure, they may have been named after the village in Massachusetts where they were cultivated, but there's no shortage of proof that Chautauqua County is grape central. The region is the oldest and largest Concord grape-growing area in the world, and it is the second largest grape-growing region in the nation. (The first is Napa Valley, California.) The Lake Erie Concord Grape Belt Area is also the first location in New York State to be named a designated agricultural heritage area.

One purveyor of Concords is the Growers' Cooperative Grape Juice Company in Westfield, whose unsweetened Concord grape concentrate was a Nickel City Chef secret ingredient. Growers' Cooperative is a grower-owned organization in the "Concord Grape Belt," a fifty-mile stretch of Concord acreage along the southern shore of Lake Erie, extending along the Alleghany Plateau Escarpment from southwestern New York to northwestern Pennsylvania. The climate along the shore of Lake Erie is perfect for growing Concords because the lake delays the autumn frost and allows the grapes to fully mature.

Growers' Cooperative began in 1929 with only eight growers. Today, more than 150 growers produce 20,000 tons of Concord grapes harvested each season from 3,000 acres of prime farmland. In the off-season, other growers utilize the Cooperative's equipment to process blueberries, cranberries, and cherries. In addition to providing a useful service to growers of these other fruits, this arrangement allows Growers' Cooperative to keep its machinery active year-round. "Concord grapes are our heritage and our passion," says Dave Momberger, general manager of Growers' Cooperative. "Today's mass-merchandised retail 100% grape juice products are no longer 100% Concord grape. At Growers', we have an ongoing initiative to preserve the identity of the Eastern Concord grape, and have developed a product that is all Concord."

Concord grapes may conjure up images of peanut butter and grape jelly sandwiches for some, but there are other more interesting uses for these delicious grapes that can be made into many value-added products, including grape juice concentrates, purées, and grape seed oil. For Nickel City Chef Challenge: Concord Grapes, the chefs were given the opportunity to use all of these unique Concord grape products.

Concord grape pie has long been a favorite recipe in the northeastern U.S., but over the years, the intense process required to skin and seed Concords has meant that many no longer make it. Fortunately, a few companies have begun to sell the grape purée, which makes this old-fashioned favorite a snap to prepare.

In addition, Concord grape juice and unsweetened Concord grape concentrate contain natural plant compounds (also called flavonoids) similar to those found in red wine, which function as antioxidants and appear to play an important role in overall health. Grape seed oil, on the other hand, does not contain as many antioxidants as grape juice or purée because most of the antioxidants are found in the grape skin. It is, however, excellent for cooking because of its high smoking point and nearly imperceptible flavor.

So, the next time you reach for a jar of grape jelly at the supermarket, read the label. Support the local economy by purchasing all-Concord jellies and juices from Growers' Cooperative. Your taste buds will know the difference.

The southernmost region of Western New York and Northeastern Pennsylvania are home to the second largest grape growing region in the United States.

48

Tempo and Aroma restaurants both focus on Italian flavors and preparations, including cooking with wine, so giving Chef Paul Jenkins from Tempo and Chef Keith Dulak from Aroma grape ingredients to cook with may seem unchallenging. However, while Concord grapes should be thought of as more than just the jelly kids prefer on their peanut butter sandwiches, using the unsweetened concentrate is nothing like cooking with wine.

Nickel City Chef was pleased to include an agricultural item that plays such an important role in the southern tier of Western New York, and each course delivered by the chefs approached this secret ingredient quite differently, some more successfully than others. Having access to both the unsweetened Concord concentrate and the sweet-as-pie Concord purée gave the chefs some flexibility, but this competition was one of the toughest challenges of the series.

Surprisingly, although grape pie has long been a favorite of bakers in regions where Concord grapes are prolific, neither chef chose to make a play on this classic dessert. Instead, they both thought outside the box, each chef presenting twists on the secret ingredient that took me and, in some cases, the judges, by surprise.

"They both truly thought outside the box, each chef presenting twists on the secret ingredient that took me and, in some cases, the judges, by surprise."

Chef Paul Jenkins prepared a visually impressive New York State-inspired caprese salad (page 51), making mozzarella from a locally produced cheese curd and garnishing the salad with microgreens from Flavor Farm. The dish was topped with preserved lemon rind and a Concord gastrique, and the combination of the two was divine, a real treat for the senses in taste, scent, and texture. Jenkins' preparation of foie gras was also delicious; his searing of the foie gave it texture and unctuousness that was perfectly complemented by the bright and savory Concord "jam" he used to dress the plate.

Chef Keith Dulak's decision to feature bone marrow was a brave one, as temperature is such an important factor in the mouth-feel and overall enjoyment of this ingredient. In mid-winter, the Nickel City Chef showroom can be a bit chilly, but Dulak took the risk anyway. The result? This dish was appreciated by our judges as one of his best.

His second course was a play on peanut butter and jelly, with a Concord reduction and little bits of peanut bringing flavor to a scallop ravioli. Overall, the judges disliked this dish, and it may be what ultimately cost him the win. His third course, featuring braised duck, was good, but he's made it even better with the revised recipe on page 50.

Both Chef Jenkins and Chef Dulak are at the helm of extremely popular and critically acclaimed Italian restaurants located not far from one another. The use of a tricky secret ingredient and the pairing of these two chefs produced a challenge so intense that the feeling easily carried over into the audience. Typically, Nickel City Chef challenges feel like the manifestation of a wager between friends. In this instance, it felt like a competition through and through.

LEI Photography

Nickel City Chef Jenkins sizes up the Wegmans pantry of fresh produce and dry goods available to both chefs.

CHALLENGE 7: CONCORD GRAPE CONCENTRATE FROM GRAPE GROWERS' COOPERATIVE

Duck Breast
with Concord Chèvre Croquette

Servings: 4 | Total prep and cooking time: 90 minutes, including marination

INGREDIENTS

4 duck breasts

1 cup Concord grape jam

1/2 cup organic red wine vinegar

1/2 cup white balsamic vinegar

1 cup bread crumbs from day-old bread

8 ounces chèvre cheese

1 large Russet potato, peeled and cubed

1 large shallot, diced

1 egg, beaten

1/2 cup vegetable oil

Extra virgin olive oil

Flour for dusting

Salt and pepper

50

DIRECTIONS

• Remove excess skin from the duck, leaving amount desired. Crosshatch skin with a sharp knife. In a large bowl, mix 1/2 cup of jam and enough wine vinegar to thin the mixture. Add duck and marinate in the refrigerator for one hour.

• Meanwhile, submerge the potato in a pot of water and bring to boil over high heat until fork tender. Remove the potato and drain. Place it in a mixing bowl with the chèvre and remaining grape purée. Blend with a wire whisk until combined. Form the potato into puck-like discs approximately 1/2 inch thick. Set aside. Prepare a small breading station with three plates, one containing the flour, another the egg, and the third, the bread crumbs.

• In a sauté pan, heat about a 1/4 inch of vegetable oil on low. Once hot, batter and bread the croquettes by lightly dredging them in flour, then dipping them in the egg, followed by breadcrumbs. Fry, turning mid-way, until crispy and golden brown on both sides. Remove the croquettes from oil and cool on a paper towel.

• Remove the duck from the marinade and pat dry with a paper towel. Season with salt and pepper. Heat a nonstick sauté pan over medium-high heat and add duck skin side down. Sear until the fat renders completely, then turn and continue for 2 minutes or until desired temperature is achieved. Remove from heat and rest.

• Quickly add the diced shallot to the duck fat remaining in the pan and sauté. As soon as it begins to go translucent, remove shallot to a small bowl and add the white balsamic vinegar and the extra virgin olive oil. Add salt and pepper to taste.

PLATING

Place the crispy croquette in the center of the plate, add the sliced duck breast, drizzle with vinaigrette. Fresh endive or wilted greens make an excellent accompaniment to this dish.

Concord Caprese
with Preserved Lemon

Nancy J. Parisi

Servings: 4 | Total prep and cooking time: 30 minutes, not including lemon preservation

INGREDIENTS

INGREDIENTS

1 1/2 pounds fresh mozzarella, cut in 1/4 inch slices

Fresh basil

Salt and pepper

8 ounces unsweetened Concord grape concentrate

12 ounces extra virgin olive oil

Fresh basil

Salt and pepper

6 to 8 lemons (depending on size)

1/2 cup kosher salt

DIRECTIONS

Concord Caprese

- In a small saucepan over medium heat, reduce grape juice concentrate by half. Remove from heat, cooling to room temperature. Whisk in the extra virgin olive oil until combined.

- Stack the fresh mozzarella and drizzle with the Concord vinaigrette.

Preserved Lemons (requires 14 to 30 days)

- Thoroughly wash the lemons. Sprinkle 1 tablespoon of salt in the bottom of a jar which has a tightly fitting lid. Make two intersecting slices in the bottom of each lemon (like an "x"), separating most of the lemon into four quarters, but without cutting all the way through; the lemon should remain attached to its base. Sprinkle approximately 1 tablespoon of salt into the cuts on each lemon. Pack the lemons into the jar, sprinkling a light dusting of salt over each layer before adding the next. More than a 1/2 cup of salt may be required. Use a wooden spoon to push the lemons down, packing them firmly. Close the jar tightly. Leave in a cool place for 30 days.

- Make sure that by day two the lemons are completely covered with juice. If necessary, squeeze the juice from one or two fresh lemons and pour into the jar; keeping the lemons covered with juice is important.

- Let them sit at room temperature for at least two weeks, shaking the jar periodically to redistribute the juice and salt. When they are ready, remove the lemons from the liquid and rinse well to remove the salt.

- Scrape out the pulp from each lemon slice. Place the lemons in a clean jar and cover with olive oil. Store them in the refrigerator for up to six months.

PLATING

Top the Concord Caprese with a preserved lemon rind or thin slivers of preserved lemon peel. Peppery greens are a lovely addition to this dish.

51

CHALLENGING CHEF
Keith Dulak
of Trattoria Aroma

Veal Bone Marrow
Seared Foie Gras, Shaved
Cantaloupe, Fig, Concord and
Gorgonzola Crostini

Scallop Thyme Ravioli
Concord Reduction, Cracked
Peppercorn, Peanut Crumbs

Braised Duck Leg
Roasted Concord, Pork Belly, Goat
Cheese, Balsamic Shallot Vinaigrette

NICKEL CITY CHEF
Paul Jenkins
of Tempo

New York State Caprese with
Hand-pulled Mozzarella
Concord Gastrique, Preserved
Lemon

Hudson Valley Foie Gras and
Diver Scallop
Sweet Pea Purée, Savory
Concord Jam, Concord Nut Bread

Pan-roasted Cervena Venison
Grape Jus, Olive Oil Potato Purée,
Sweet Marsala Reduction

SCORES FOR CHALLENGE 7

	Challenging Chef Keith Dulak		Nickel City Chef Paul Jenkins
Taste & Flavor	10	Taste & Flavor	11
Creativity	11	Creativity	11
Plating & Presentation	10	Plating & Presentation	10
Technical Execution	8	Technical Execution	11
Use of Secret Ingredient	10	Use of Secret Ingredient	10
Audience Vote	1	Audience Vote	0
Total	**50**		**53**

The Challenger:
Keith Dulak
Trattoria Aroma
307 Bryant Street, Buffalo
thearomagroup.com

Keith Dulak grew up on Buffalo's West Side, leaving home to attend Paul Smith's College in

> When Dulak learned that Aroma would open a second location in the city, just blocks from his childhood neighborhood, he gladly accepted.

the Adirondacks. The itch to travel found him moving to Northern California within the year, looking for a different perspective on cooking.

He later returned to finish his degree at Paul Smith's, and upon graduation he chose to

bring his passion for cooking back home to Buffalo. After three years of working as a sous at Aroma's successful Williamsville location, he was promoted to executive chef. When Dulak learned that Aroma would open a second location in the city, just blocks from his childhood neighborhood, he gladly accepted the offer to become the new executive chef.

Trattoria Aroma quickly became one of the city's most highly rated restaurants, focusing on farm fresh ingredients, a *Wine Spectator* award-winning wine list, and one of the most consistently delicious dining experiences in Western New York. Dulak holds down the bustling kitchen, where he pushes himself to learn more every day.

CHALLENGE 8

Balaton Cherries

FROM SINGER FARM NATURALS

 VS.

Nickel City Chef
Krista Van Wagner
Curly's, Lackawanna, NY

Challenging Chef
Andrew Nuernberger
The Roycroft Inn
East Aurora, NY

Singer Farm Naturals

Appleton, New York   singerfarmnaturals.com

The beautiful and breezy Lake Ontario shoreline is the picturesque locale of Singer Farms, a fifth-generation, 500-acre farm located in Appleton, New York. Vivianne Singer Szulist and her husband, Thomas Szulist, operate Singer Farm Naturals on twenty-two acres of property purchased from Vivianne's family and affiliated with the farm. While the original Singer Farms is well-known for its annual crop of fresh fruit, Singer Farms Naturals (SFN) is focused on the retail side of farming. Together, Viv and Tom, who have been married since 2009, have developed a product line for retail sale that takes advantage of the family's access to fresh Niagara County fruit.

Singer Farm Naturals' products include dried diced apples and a variety of dried cherries that are excellent for baking and cooking. They are even better when served up in SFN's signature style, which includes dipping them in chocolate and yogurt. Singer's Balaton cherries were the secret ingredient of Nickel City Chef's eighth battle, with both dried and frozen versions of this crimson tart fruit available to the competing chefs. Each used the Balatons in a broad variety of ways.

Balaton cherries are a large and firm variety of cherry developed in the mid-1980s by Michigan State University and commercially released in the mid-1990s. Since then, Balatons have become a popular varietal in New York and other cherry-growing states. Their deep, rich color and firmness make them a favorite of pastry chefs.

Tom and Viv continue to add new products under the umbrella of their brand, and their efforts to develop a specialty gourmet brand using locally raised produce means that Western New Yorkers now have access to delicious dried local fruits year-round. In addition to the tart Balaton cherry, Singer Farms also grows the tart Montmorency cherry, along with six

varieties of sweet cherries, three varieties of quince, two varieties of pears, four varieties of apricots, ten varieties of peaches, and twenty varieties each of apples and plums. The most recent SFN additions are an amazing tart cherry juice and Tom's latest obsession– garlic. He now grows more than twenty-two specialty varieties of the pungent bulb.

Since settling onto their property, the Szulists have undertaken a project that is so unusual it has been reported in several newspapers. The couple's efforts to rehabilitate their Civil War-era barn and convert it into a green building is also documented on Viv's blog, "Old Barn, New Life." Now that the barn rehab is complete, the couple have opened it to the public as a retail outlet for the increasing variety of products they grow and produce–especially those tart cherries.

In addition to their unique line of dried fruits, the Szulists grow dozens of varieties of garlic on their Niagara County farm.

This challenge, which took place in early April, was the first in which fruit was used as the Nickel City Chef secret ingredient. April is a time of year when most Western New Yorkers might consider accessing local fruit difficult, so I hoped that by selecting Balaton cherries from Singer Farm Naturals as the secret ingredient, the audience would discover otherwise. In regions of the world fortunate enough to have four seasons, preservation methods such as freezing and drying are ideal ways to make use of a harvest through the winter and well into the spring.

This challenge was interesting because it pitted two chefs of longstanding Western New York establishments against one another. The Roycroft Inn, arguably the best-recognized building on the Roycroft Campus, is an historical establishment at the center of the nation's Arts & Crafts movement. Curly's, owned and operated by Nickel City Chef Krista Van Wagner and her husband, Kirk, has been feeding Buffalonians for more than seventy-five years. As expected, both chefs held up well under the pressure of competing in front of a captivated audience.

> *"April is a time of year when most Western New Yorkers might consider it difficult to access local fruit, so I hoped that by selecting Balaton cherries from Singer Farm Naturals as the secret ingredient, the audience would discover this to be untrue."*

Roycroft Chef Andrew Nuernberger did a good job of presenting the judges with dishes that represent the style of cuisine typically served at the Roycroft. Each simple and approachable dish accentuated the use of local specialty ingredients. He and his sous chef worked congruously and neatly, completing everything on time and with confidence. His incorporation of the Balaton cherries in his second and third courses made sense within the context of each dish. Unfortunately, in his first course, which featured lobster, vanilla sauce, and oyster mushrooms, the cherries felt like an afterthought.

Conversely, Nickel City Chef Van Wagner left her Caribbean roots at home and presented a series of offerings that largely impressed the judges in presentation, technical ability, and flavor. Her first course, a cherry and bacon biscuit topped with foie gras, quail egg, and cherry gastrique, did an excellent job of appealing to their palates. Each bite provided a complex blend of saltiness, sweetness, fat, smoke, and richness. Another winner was Van Wagner's dessert (page 57) which married springy white cake, light-as-air vanilla mousse, and a sweet cherry compote with watercress, an unexpected and peppery garnish.

Judge Ivy Knight, a well-known Toronto food writer and former chef, may have summed up this challenge best. In our discussion after the show, she said that while she was impressed with team Roycroft's ability to work together and to remain calm under pressure, the perfectly synched Van Wagner duo worked together so seamlessly that they were nearly impossible to beat.

Nickel City Chef Van Wagner prepares the dough for her Cherry Bacon Biscuit.

55

CHALLENGE 8: BALATON CHERRIES FROM SINGER FARM NATURALS

Spice-rubbed Rack of Lamb
with Balaton Chutney

Servings: 6 | Total prep and cooking time: 1 hour | Preheat grill to 400°F

INGREDIENTS

1 2-pound rack of lamb, frenched
1/2 cup olive oil
1 teaspoon kosher salt
1 teaspoon black pepper
1 teaspoon ground fennel seed
1 piece star anise, crushed
1 teaspoon ground coriander
1/2 teaspoon ground cumin

1 cup red onion, minced
1/2 cup granulated sugar
1/2 cup red wine vinegar
1 tablespoon garlic, minced
1 teaspoon ground cinnamon
1 teaspoon ground cumin
1/2 teaspoon ground nutmeg
1 teaspoon crushed red pepper flakes
1 pound dried Balaton cherries
1/2 cup cherry juice

DIRECTIONS

Lamb

• Combine all spices and set aside. Massage 1 ounce of olive oil into the meat. Then rub the spice mixture into the meat, creating a crust. Let rest at room temperature for one hour.

• Place the seasoned lamb on the 400°F grill, searing it for about 2 minutes on all sides. Turn the grill to low heat and cook until the lamb reaches 145°F internally. Turn the lamb consistently to prevent burning.

Chutney

• Sauté the red onion in one ounce of olive oil until tender. Add the sugar and dissolve. Add the cherries, ginger, garlic, cinnamon, cumin, nutmeg, and pepper flakes, and sauté for 2 minutes until heated through. Add the vinegar and cherry juice, reducing until almost dry. This may be served hot or at room temperature with the lamb.

56

PLATING

This dish is best served with roasted Yukon Gold potatoes and sautéed fennel. For a restaurant-style presentation, pool the chutney on the plate, topping it with two chops. Garnish with fennel sprigs for color.

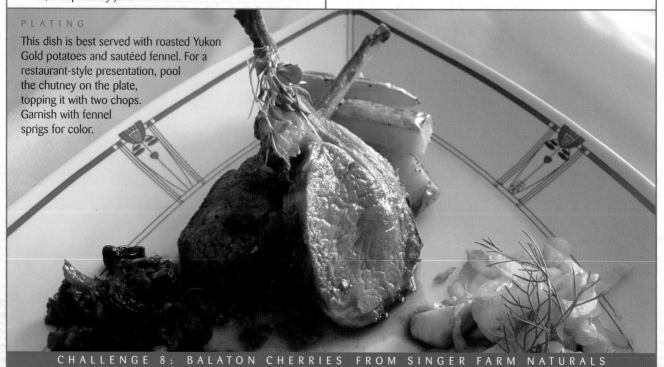

Nancy J. Parisi

Vanilla Bean Mascarpone Mousse
with Balaton Compote

Servings: 6 | Total prep and cooking time: 1 hour (resets in refrigerator overnight)

INGREDIENTS

1 cup half and half
1/2 cup mascarpone
1 tablespoon New York State honey
1 vanilla bean
1 egg white
1/3 cup sugar
1/2 cup heavy cream

DIRECTIONS

Mousse

• Cut the vanilla bean in half and scrape the seeds from the interior of one half. Place the seeds and half of the bean pod into a sauce pan with the half and half. Warm over low heat until it just begins to bubble. Remove from heat and let cool.

• Combine the mascarpone and honey. Add 2 tablespoons of cooled vanilla bean cream. Set aside. Add heavy cream to a chilled bowl. Scrape remaining half of the vanilla bean into the cream and whisk until it forms soft peaks. Refrigerate until chilled.

• Whip the egg whites and sugar until they form a glossy, loose meringue. Gently fold in the mascarpone and honey mixture. Once combined, fold in the whipped cream gently. Refrigerate overnight.

2 star anise, whole
2 cloves, whole
1 tablespoon white peppercorns, whole
4 tablespoons unsalted butter
1 cup dried Balaton cherries
1 cinnamon stick
1/3 cup New York State honey
1 teaspoon orange zest
2 ounces Kirschwasser (cherry brandy)

Compote

• Grind the star anise, cloves, and white peppercorns together until they become a fine powder. Measure one teaspoon of the spice powder and reserve the remainder in an airtight jar for later use.

• Melt the butter in a sauce pan, along with one teaspoon of spice powder, cherries, honey, and cinnamon stick. Deglaze the pan with Kirschwasser brandy and simmer 5 minutes. Cool.

PLATING

This mousse can be molded into a large ring and turned out on a plate with the compote served on the side for presentation, or spooned into individual dishes and topped with the cherry compote. Chef Van Wagner wowed the judges by serving it with delicate white cake and garnishing with a small amount of peppery micro watercress from Flavor Farm.

CHALLENGING CHEF
Andrew Nuernberger
of the Roycroft Inn

NICKEL CITY CHEF
Krista Van Wagner
of Curly's

Vanilla-poached Canadian Lobster, Vanilla Cream, Dried Cherry Reduction, Oyster Mushrooms

Cherry-Bacon Biscuit with Foie Gras Quail Egg, Cherry Gastrique, Popcorn Shoots

Spice-crusted Rack of Lamb with Cherry Chutney, Roasted Potatoes, Sautéed Fennel

Roasted Quail Cherry Reduction, Sweet Potato Frites, Cherry Mango Couscous

Balaton Cherry Chocolate Mousse, Cherry Sauce, Chocolate Cherry Pecan Cookie

Vanilla Mascarpone Mousse White Cake, Cherry Compote, Watercress

58

SCORES FOR CHALLENGE 8

	Challenging Chef Andrew Nuernberger		Nickel City Chef Krista Van Wagner
Taste & Flavor	9	Taste & Flavor	11
Creativity	8	Creativity	10
Plating & Presentation	9	Plating & Presentation	11
Technical Execution	8	Technical Execution	11
Use of Secret Ingredient	8	Use of Secret Ingredient	9
Audience Vote	0	Audience Vote	1
Total	**42**		**53**

The Challenger:
Chef Andrew Nuernberger
The Roycroft Inn
40 South Grove Street, East Aurora
roycroftinn.com

Andrew Nuernberger is the executive chef of a true Western New York treasure, the Roycroft Inn. A National Historic Landmark, the Inn is part of the East Aurora-based Arts & Crafts campus founded by Elbert Hubbard in 1895. This campus became the hub of the Roycroft movement, which had tremendous influence on American design and architecture in the early twentieth century.

> He believes dining is a total experience, from the ambiance of the restaurant and service, to the food that is served.

The Roycroft remained a mecca for great thinkers, artists, and students of the movement until 1938. In 1986 it was granted landmark status and was fully refurbished through the efforts of many, reopening in 1995 and becoming recognized for its stunning architecture and quiet luxury.

Inspired by the Inn's history of artistry and creation, chef Nuernberger takes a contemporary approach to the bountiful regional and seasonal ingredients that are available throughout the year. He believes that dining is a total experience, from the ambiance of the restaurant and service provided, to the food that is served. Under this philosophy, all must excel and complement in order to be remembered and revisited.

CHALLENGE 9

Maple

FROM BALDWIN HILL FARMS

 VS.

Nickel City Chef
Adam Goetz
Sample, Buffalo, NY

Challenging Chef
Steven Gedra
Bistro Europa, Buffalo, NY

Baldwin Hill Farms

Rushford, New York   maplelady.com

Most know her affectionately as "The Maple Lady," the force behind the many products produced from fresh New York State maple syrup on Baldwin Hills Farms.

Bonnie Yox operates the farm along with her husband, Paul, and son, Brandon, developing new products like salad dressings and sauces. Each year, their small maple shack is flooded with visitors eager to try these new concoctions, as well as the more classic offerings of maple syrup and maple-infused candy. The popularity of maple products in Western New York meant it was only a matter of time before Nickel City Chef came calling for a secret ingredient.

Bonnie and Paul Yox originally lived in the southern part of the state before retiring to Florida. But after thirteen years, the couple returned to Western New York and began "sugaring" as a hobby. Today, they produce several maple-inspired products, including the rarely seen maple vinegar.

While the couple's inventiveness may be rare, their passion for maple syrup is not. New York State is the fourth-largest producer of maple syrup worldwide—more than 250,000 gallons each year. It is a state lush with maple trees, most of which remain untapped, perhaps because it takes nearly forty gallons of maple sap to make one delicious gallon of syrup. Despite the hard work required to render this amazing elixir from its forests, Western New York is home to nearly 100 maple producers. And as the thousands of visitors who have had stopped by Baldwin Hill Farm's Sugar House at "boiling time" in February and March can attest, seeing the maple sugar process from start to finish is truly fascinating.

The use of maple sap in New York State can be traced to Native Americans, who first taught settlers how to tap and make maple syrup. It is a proud part of our country's edible history and an important commodity in New York. Sadly, most of the commercially available pancake and waffle syrups sold today are a poor imitation—many contain no real maple syrup at all.

In addition to the flavor sacrifice, this also represents a regrettable nutritional loss, since real maple syrup is an excellent source of calcium and can be used as a natural sweetener in many culinary applications. (For more information about New York State's maple legacy, visit nysmaple.com.)

In Nickel City Chef's ninth challenge, Baldwin Hill Farms provided the two competing chefs with quarts of maple syrup, pounds of fresh granulated maple sugar, and pints of maple vinegar, giving them plenty of culinary options and their creations plenty of flavor.

BALDWIN HILL FARMS
Pure Maple Products
and
Gourmet Foods
585-437-2106

OPEN HOUSE!
MAPLE WEEKEND
MARCH 20-21
MARCH 27-28
10AM to 4PM

Known as "The Maple Lady," Bonnie Yox is the heart and soul of her family's maple business.

60

Most everyone enjoys sweets, but professional food judges and wine tasters know that sweet flavors can alter your palate, making it hard for you to appreciate and suss out other important flavor notes. So asking our chefs to cook six courses featuring maple syrup was asking a great deal.

For competitors Nickel City Chef Adam Goetz of Sample and challenger Steven Gedra of Bistro Europa to impress the judges, they would need to find a way to make sure that the characteristics of maple were present in each dish without masking other aspects of the preparation or the course following it. Fortunately, Baldwin Hill Farms makes a unique maple vinegar that is more vinegar than maple, giving the chefs some savory options. Both chefs, however, still felt that maple flavor should be present in each course.

Pairing these two chefs in a face off was exciting because they couldn't have been more different. While both received their culinary education in the kitchen rather than at school, Goetz is a detail-driven chef whose restaurant is known for its diminutive creative interpretations of classic dishes. Working on this scale, Goetz is careful, conscientious, and a stickler for perfection. He has a particular talent for plating and, as a Nickel City Chef, typically pulls in high marks in this category.

Gedra, on the other hand, is all about flavor, and his cavalier attitude and passion for highlighting fine ingredients shines in each dish. When asked whether he misses working in a fine-dining setting, Gedra once told me he was all done peeling tiny carrots and cooking ten peas at a time. His dishes are typically plated with little flair, but he excels at building flavor into them and this occasion was no exception.

> *"Fortunately, Baldwin Hill Farms makes a unique maple vinegar that is more vinegar than maple, giving the chefs some savory options."*

Nowhere were the competitors' differences more pronounced than in their first course. While Goetz's offering featured an intensely technical four-component maple progression, which highlighted the myriad ways in which the secret ingredient could be transformed, Gedra's was a flavor bomb of smoky, salty pork belly, a rich poached egg coated in crispy tempura batter, truffled potatoes, and maple vinaigrette.

In the end, both chefs received high marks. The audience displayed great enthusiasm for the chefs and the types of food they were preparing, and the tension inherent in watching closely matched competitors was compelling from start to finish. As always, Goetz brought flavor, precision, and a studied approach to the table, tying Gedra's efforts at nearly every step.

In the end, Chef Gedra prevailed despite his rejection of "fancy pants" presentation. His successful use of the secret ingredient, adventuresome nature, and maple bacon milkshake earned him the win.

Nickel City Chef Goetz and his sous, James Gehrke, work to turn maple syrup and maple sugar into several impressive courses, including a four component "Maple Tasting."

CHALLENGING CHEF STEVEN GEDRA'S
Maple-crusted Venison
with Crispy Braising Greens and Maple Vinegar

Servings: 6 | Total prep and cooking time: 1 hour (not including marination process) | Preheat oven to 300°F

INGREDIENTS

3 pounds venison, cleaned of any silverskin or sinew*

1 cup B grade maple syrup

1 3/4 cups vegetable oil

1/4 cup olive oil

10 Tellicherry peppercorns

5 juniper berries

10 coriander seeds

10 cumin seeds

3 bay leaves

5 allspice berries

5 cardamom pods

2 black kokum

1 bulb garlic, smashed

2 shallots, chopped

20 stems fresh thyme, whole

20 stems fresh sage, whole

20 stems fresh rosemary, whole

*We use Denver Leg at the restaurant, but any tender cut such as loin, chop, or rack will suffice.

DIRECTIONS

Venison

- Toast the peppercorns, juniper, coriander seed, cumin seed, bay leaf, allspice, cardamom, and kokum in a sauté pan over medium heat until aromatic. Remove from heat and place on a plate to cool. In a double boiler, combine the maple syrup, oil, toasted spices, garlic, shallot, and herbs. Heat over medium heat for about 10 minutes or until viscous. Cool the maple and oil mixture to room temperature and pour over the cleaned venison. Marinate in the refrigerator for at least 24 hours (ideally 48 to 72 hours). Remove the venison from the marinade and dry with paper towels. Season with salt and black pepper.

- Lightly brown 3 tablespoons of unsalted butter in a large pan. Sear the venison on all sides, basting with a spoon the entire time, until the meat becomes rare.
Note: Venison is very lean and dries out very quickly. This meat cooked more than medium rare will become tough and inedible.

- Set the meat on a rack and tightly pack the streusel on each piece. Cook in a 300°F oven for about 5 to 7 minutes.

- Set the meat on a rack to rest for 5 to 10 minutes.
Slice to serve.

---

3 tablespoons unsalted butter

1/2 pound maple sugar

1/4 pound unsalted butter, room temperature

Pinch of salt

1/4 tablespoon fresh thyme, chopped

1/4 tablespoon fresh sage, chopped

1/2 teaspoon ground cumin, toasted

1/2 teaspoon ground coriander, toasted

Streusel

- Combine the streusel ingredients in a bowl and mix well, pinching with your fingers to incorporate the butter until you have a smooth, homogeneous mixture. Set aside at room temperature.

---

1 pound braising greens (kale, Swiss chard, dandelion, komatsunu, etc.), washed and dried

1/2 tablespoon blended oil

1 tablespoon maple vinegar

1/8 tablespoon fresh thyme, chopped

1/8 tablespoon fresh sage, chopped

Salt and pepper

Greens

- Place a large sauté pan over high heat. Add the oil until it shimmers, just before it starts to smoke. Add the thyme and sage. Quickly add the greens, applying pressure to them with a spatula or a smaller pan. Cook until they become wilted and brown. Deglaze the pan with the maple vinegar. Add salt and pepper to taste, combining thoroughly.

PLATING Fan slices of venison over whipped sweet potatoes or roasted yellow potatoes. Serve with greens on the side. Garnish with finely chopped chives.

Maple-braised Short Ribs
with Soft Polenta, Pickled Asparagus, and Butternut Vinaigrette

Servings: 4 | Total prep and cooking time: 2 hours | Preheat oven to 350°F

2 pounds beef short ribs
3 cups maple syrup
1 1/2 cups red wine
3 roma tomatoes, chopped
3 stalks celery, chopped
2 carrots, peeled and chopped
1 red onion, chopped
8 cloves garlic, chopped
2 bay leaves
3 sprigs rosemary
Canola oil

DIRECTIONS
Maple Braised Short Ribs

• Put chopped celery, carrots, onion, and garlic in a bowl. Heat a heavy-bottomed Dutch oven on medium-high. Add 2 or 3 tablespoons of canola oil to the pan. Season the short ribs with salt and sear them on both sides. Once caramelized, remove the ribs from the pan and set them aside. Lower the heat to medium and add the vegetables and rosemary, cooking until tender. Add the tomatoes and cook approximately 10 minutes, or until the pan becomes dry. Add the red wine, cooking for 10 more minutes. Put the ribs back in the pan along with the maple syrup and just enough water to cover them. Cover the pan with foil and place in the oven for 1 1/2 hours, or until the meat is tender.

1 bunch asparagus
1 1/4 cup maple vinegar
1 cup maple sugar
2 tablespoons kosher salt
1 cup water
2 tablespoons crushed red pepper flakes

Pickled Asparagus

• Use a peeler to slice the asparagus into thin ribbons. Put the ribbons in a bowl and set aside. Bring all the other ingredients to a boil in a small pot. Taste, and adjust for spiciness, sweetness, and acidity with pepper flakes, sugar, or vinegar. Pour the liquid over the asparagus ribbons and cover the bowl with plastic wrap. Set aside.

1 quart unsalted chicken broth
1 cup coarsely ground corn meal
3 tablespoons unsalted butter
1 1/2 teaspoons kosher salt
6 ounces Manchego cheese, shredded

Soft Polenta

• In a medium sauce pan, simmer the chicken stock and salt. Add corn meal and reduce heat to low. Using a whisk, stir the polenta vigorously and constantly so it does not stick or burn. Once the corn meal has absorbed all the stock, it should be tender. If not, add a bit more stock or warm water and continue cooking. When the corn meal is done, remove from the heat and stir in the cheese and butter. Season with salt and pepper to taste.

1 yellow onion, sliced
4 cloves garlic, crushed
1 butternut squash, diced
2 ounces rice wine vinegar
2 ounces canola oil

Butternut Squash Vinaigrette

• In a sauce pan, cook the onion and garlic in a little canola oil until tender. Add the diced squash and continue to cook for 5 minutes. Add enough water to cover the squash by about an inch. Season with salt and pepper and let simmer until squash is tender. Pour mixture into a blender and add rice wine vinegar. Purée until smooth. With the blender still running, slowly add the oil. Season with salt and pepper to taste.

PLATING

Spoon polenta onto the center of a plate. Top with slices of short rib and asparagus ribbons. Drizzle the vinaigrette around the outside and over the top of the stack, providing adequate moisture and additional color to the dish.

63

CHALLENGING CHEF
Steven Gedra
of Bistro Europa

"Grand Slam:"
• Maple-glazed Smoked Pork Belly
• Truffled Potato Ramp Hash
• Tempura Fried Egg
• Maple Vinaigrette

Maple-crusted Venison
Whipped Sweet Potato, Crispy Braised
Greens, Natural Jus

Foie Gras and Lingonberry PBJ
Maple Bacon Milkshake

NICKEL CITY CHEF
Adam Goetz
of Sample

Maple Tasting:
• Bruléed Grapefruit Supreme
  with Mint and Maple
• Poached Egg, Toast Crumbles,
  and Whipped Maple Butter
• Crispy Maple-Syrup-braised
  Pork Belly with Arugula Salad
• Brewed Coffee with Maple Cream Foam

Maple-braised Short Ribs
Manchego Soft Polenta, Spicy Pickled
Asparagus, Butternut Vinaigrette

Bread Pudding of Warm Buttermilk
Waffles
Maple Syrup Fennel Oil, Macerated
Berries, Candied Walnuts

64

SCORES FOR CHALLENGE 9

	Challenging Chef Steven Gedra		Nickel City Chef Adam Goetz
Taste & Flavor	12	Taste & Flavor	12
Creativity	11	Creativity	11
Plating & Presentation	11	Plating & Presentation	11
Technical Execution	11	Technical Execution	11
Use of Secret Ingredient	12	Use of Secret Ingredient	8
Audience Vote	1	Audience Vote	0
Total	**58**		**53**

The Challenger:
Chef Steven Gedra
Bistro Europa
484 Elmwood Avenue, Buffalo
europabuffalo.com

Like many of Western New York's talented young chefs, Steven Gedra left Buffalo looking for greener pastures and a big-city restaurant experience. He found himself in Boston, in the kitchen of the highly rated Blu. From there he bounced around a bit, spending time cooking at the Larkspur in Vail, Colorado, before becoming a private chef for an affluent Boston family that is part owner of the Boston Celtics.

While many restaurant chefs tend to wither under the constraints of cooking privately for a family, Gedra's circumstances were unique. The family he worked for hosted magnificent parties for charity, at which famous chefs from all over North America would lend their skills. Gedra was able to cook alongside—and in some cases, befriend—renowned chefs like Eric Ripert, Daniel Boulud, Sam Mason, Ming Tsai, Michael Schlow, and Susur Lee.

In January 2010, Gedra and his wife, Ellen, a talented pastry chef, purchased Bistro Europa. In just a short time, they earned the hearts of Buffalo's most passionate diners.

Gedra was able to cook alongside—and in some cases, befriend—renowned chefs like Eric Ripert, Daniel Boulud, Sam Mason, Ming Tsai, Michael Schlow, and Susur Lee.

CHALLENGE 10

Wine

FROM ARROWHEAD SPRING VINEYARDS

VS.

Nickel City Chef
JJ Richert
Torches, Buffalo, NY

Challenging Chef
Dino DeBell
Blue Monk, Buffalo, NY

Arrowhead Spring Vineyards

Cambria, NY   arrowheadspringvineyards.com

Duncan Ross began making wine to prove to his wife, Robin, that his dream of starting a vineyard was realistic. This eventually led to Arrowhead Spring Vineyards in Cambria, New York, one of the newest members of the Niagara Wine Trail–and the makers of the secret ingredient used in Nickel City Chef's tenth challenge.

Although Arrowhead only began making wine in 2005, Duncan and Robin Rosses' love for wine began many years earlier. The Rosses have been taking wine-related vacations, including their honeymoon in Sonoma County, California, for two decades. When Duncan was crowned National Amateur Wine Champion in 2002 at the Indy Competition, the largest international amateur wine competition in North America, the couple decided they had the proof they had sought–Duncan's dream was realistic, after all. So they started looking for land and eventually bought twenty-five acres in Niagara County. Arrowhead Spring now produces a wide selection of wines from the grapes grown in its biodynamic vineyard.

The biodynamic approach views the vineyard as an ecosystem and seeks to maintain a balance among all its facets. Techniques used at Arrowhead Spring include keeping a cover crop between rows to prevent erosion and add nitrogen back into the soil naturally, as well as playing recorded distress calls of local birds to deter actual birds from eating the grapes. Another interesting and environmentally friendly element is its location. The winery is built into the side of a hill, where the natural insulation of the earth keeps the barrel room at a constant 55 to 60°F year-round without artificial heating or cooling.

Best of all, these forward-thinking techniques and systems produce some of the region's finest wines. In recent years, Arrowhead has been awarded points by *Wine Spectator* for its 2008 Estate Syrah (87), its 2007 and 2008 Vidal Ice Wine (92 and 89, respectively), and its 2006 Chardonnay (86). Nickel City Chef's tenth challenge featured Arrowhead's Ice Wine, Meritage, and Chardonnay, all of which proved to be as excellent in recipes as they are to sip.

Meritage wines are red and white Bordeaux-style wines that were trademarked by a group of

winemakers in Napa Valley in 1988. The Meritage Alliance ensures that wines produced under this mantle do not infringe on the French Bordeaux region's legally protected rights. In order to be labeled Meritage, a red wine must contain at least two of any of these varieties: Cabernet Sauvignon, Merlot, Cabernet Franc, Petit Verdot, Malbec, St. Macaire, Gros Verdot, or Carmenere. No one varietal can comprise more than 90 percent of the blend.

Chardonnay is one of the most widely recognized varietals in the world; it is a white wine made from green-skinned Chardonnay grapes, believed to have originated in the Burgundy region of France. In fact, Chardonnay grapes are grown practically everywhere that wine is produced. Not all Chardonnay wines are the same, however, because grapes are very impressionable and clearly reflect the *terroir* and the winemaking process.

Arrowhead's award-winning ice wine is a Vidal, made by selecting grapes left on the vine well into the cold weather. In the Niagara region–an area particularly suited to the production of ice wines–the grapes are harvested early in the morning, when the temperature is ideal for picking. This method allows residual sugar to develop in the fruit, rendering a sweet dessert wine full of complex flavor notes.

Creating these wines properly takes time and dedication. As the Arrowhead Spring Vineyard mission statement makes clear, winemaking is truly a labor of love for this ambitious couple: "We will produce wines that reflect the thoughtfully chosen soils and climates from which they emanate. We will respect our surroundings, maintain good stewardship of the land, uphold our commitment to the principles of sustainable farming, and seek a deeper understanding of the natural living systems around us."

The Rosses' ability to produce dry, restaurant-quality wines using sustainable methods is unparalleled in the Western New York region.

I thought it would be impossible to convince Chef Dino DeBell to compete in a Nickel City Chef challenge. We had met on only one or two occasions, but his reputation preceded him. It would be difficult to find a successful fine-dining restaurant in Buffalo where he had not graced the kitchen at one time, but he is also a chef who has kept a low profile and avoided the spotlight.

His résumé unquestionably qualified him for a spot among our second season challengers, and the fact that restaurateur Mike Shatzel, one of Buffalo's most passionate beer enthusiasts, had hired him to develop the menu for the soon-to-open Blue Monk didn't hurt either. Knowing DeBell's personality, I honestly thought that asking him to participate would be a waste of time. But I have learned that it never hurts to ask.

So I called him and we scheduled a time to meet at Cole's, one of Buffalo's favorite neighborhood taverns, owned and operated by the Shatzel family. DeBell had been cooking there for a while, taking advantage of the fact that, unlike nearly every other chef in the city, he had the flexibility to go home evenings and enjoy time with his wife and young daughter.

To my surprise, DeBell was excited by the idea of competing and wanted to lend his support to Nickel City Chef. A proponent of sourcing fresh, local ingredients from area farms, for years DeBell has foraged for ramps, morels, and other ingredients in the wilds of Western New York. His passion for fresh, delicious food is downright contagious, and we were thrilled to have him join us.

His competitor, Nickel City Chef JJ Richert, is no less enthusiastic, and a challenge featuring the wine of one of Western New York's best wineries gave both chefs a chance to really demonstrate their skills. Arrowhead Spring Vineyards supplied three types of wine: Ice Wine, Meritage, and Chardonnay, and both chefs worked to find unexpected ways in which to use them.

"A proponent of sourcing fresh, local ingredients from area farms, for years DeBell has gone out foraging for ramps, morels, and other wild ingredients."

The first course prepared by both chefs featured the best dishes of all, and we've included their recipes (see pages 68 and 69). In the second course, Richert's daring plating choice, which included a charred octopus tentacle twisted around a vertical skewer, meant that the food arrived a little cold to the judges' table. But Chef DeBell also had difficulty. While his morel risotto was perfect and nicely complemented by ramps, his rabbit was as tough as leather.

Nickel City Chef Richert uses a molecular gastronomy technique to turn wine into "caviar" beads to garnish his Chardonnay sorbet.

Finally, in the dessert course, Richert experienced some last-minute technical difficulties when he realized that his ice cream had not frozen due to the ice cream machine's placement next to the 500°F stove. But, at the last minute, he was able to freeze his Chardonnay sorbet with the help of some dry ice. His creative take on dessert proved more impressive to our judges than DeBell's ice wine-infused pound cake.

In the end, Richert and DeBell were impressed with the quality of the wine Arrowhead produces. While Western New York has many good wineries, few are producing restaurant-quality wines. Robin and Duncan Ross have worked hard to bring our region delicious, award-winning wines, and Nickel City Chef was excited to be able to showcase them to the audience and the judges in such a unique forum.

Monkfish and Chardonnay Butter Sauce

Servings: 4 | Total prep and cooking time: 45 minutes | Preheat oven to 350°F

INGREDIENTS

1 1/2 pounds monkfish filet, cleaned

2 eggs

1/2 cup flour

1 cup fish stock

1/2 cup Arrowhead Chardonnay

1 bay leaf

7 black peppercorns

1 cup cold butter, cubed

1 bunch fresh chives

1/2 cup extra virgin olive oil

1/4 teaspoon salt

DIRECTIONS

Monkfish

• In a saucepan over medium heat, combine the stock, bay leaf, peppercorns, and wine. Reduce by three quarters. Whisk in 1/2 of the butter slowly until sauce is combined and glossy. Hold at a low temperature.

• Dredge the fish in egg and coat with flour. Set aside. Heat an ovenproof sauté pan. Add several cubes of butter. Once the butter is hot, add the fish. Sauté until it is golden on both sides. Finish in the oven for about 10 minutes.

Chive Oil

• Fill a small saucepan with water and bring to a boil. Ready an ice bath. Add the chives to the boiling water and blanch for 10 seconds. Remove and quickly plunge into the ice bath to stop the cooking process. Dry the chives on a paper towel, squeezing them gently to remove excess liquid. Once they are completely dry, cut them into 1" lengths. Put them in a blender or food processor. Add the salt. Add the olive oil in a slow and steady motion. Continue to blend until smooth. Chill at least three hours. Strain through a fine-meshed sieve, and transfer to a squirt bottle or other air-tight container. This method can also be used with ramps when they are in season.

PLATING

This dish is best served with warm, soft, new potatoes. Pool the sauce in the bottom of a plate, arrange potatoes and fish in the center. Garnish with chives or fresh, mild greens, such as red leaf lettuce.

68

NICKEL CITY CHEF JJ RICHERT'S
Meritage-braised Veal Cheeks

Nancy J. Parisi

Servings: 8 | Total prep and cooking time: 3 1/2 hours | Preheat oven to 350°F

INGREDIENTS

8 4-ounce veal cheeks, cleaned and trimmed

1 red onion, chopped

1 carrot, chopped

1 celery rib, chopped

2 cups Arrowhead Meritage Red

3 cups veal or beef stock

1/4 cup olive oil

1/4 teaspoon coriander

1/4 teaspoon fennel seed

1/2 teaspoon thyme

Salt and pepper

DIRECTIONS

• In a heavy, ovenproof dish, heat olive oil. Brown veal on both sides. Remove and set aside. Stir in the vegetables. Cook until soft. Remove meat and vegetables from the pan. Add the wine and reduce by half. Add the stock.

• Return veal to the pot and season. Bring to a simmer and cover. Once warm, move meat to the oven and braise for approximately 3 hours. Check for doneness with a fork; the veal should have a soft, melting consistency. Remove veal and set aside.

• Strain the braising liquid and place in a small saucepan on low heat. Reduce until only a 1/2 cup remains, skimming fat from the top while cooking.

69

PLATING
Serve the veal with mashed potatoes and braised carrots. Drizzle with the Meritage reduction for color and flavor. If veal cheeks are hard to source, consider using shanks.

CHALLENGE 10: WINE FROM ARROWHEAD SPRING VINEYARDS

CHALLENGING CHEF
Dino DeBell
of Blue Monk

NICKEL CITY CHEF
JJ Richert
of Torches

Monkfish with Chardonnay Butter Sauce, Warm Potato Salad, Chardonnay Butter Sauce, Wild Ramp Oil

Meritage-braised Veal Cheek with Meritage Stilton Mashed Potato, and Caramelized Carrot
Oak Barrel-smoked Chilean Sea Bass with Lemon Risotto Chardonnay Beurre Blanc

Rabbit Involtini
Foie Gras, Wild Ramp Greens, Ramp Bulb Agrodolce, Meritage Morel Risotto

Chargrilled Octopus with Heirloom Tomato Sauce
Bison, Herb, and Meritage Sausage, Maple Meritage Reduction

Ice Wine Pound Cake
Seasonal Berries, Meritage Syrup, Dark Chocolate

Chardonnay Sorbet
Meritage "Caviar," Arrowhead Cracker

SCORES FOR CHALLENGE 10

	Challenging Chef Dino DeBell		Nickel City Chef JJ Richert
Taste & Flavor	10	Taste & Flavor	9
Creativity	10	Creativity	11
Plating & Presentation	8	Plating & Presentation	10
Technical Execution	9	Technical Execution	12
Use of Secret Ingredient	11	Use of Secret Ingredient	9
Audience Vote	0	Audience Vote	1
Total	**48**		**52**

The Challenger:
Chef Dino DeBell
Blue Monk
727 Elmwood Avenue, Buffalo
Bluemonkbuffalo.com

Dino DeBell grew up around food, working at a young age for his uncle's Denver-based gourmet import company and in the kitchen of his family's restaurant. With a passion for quality ingredients and simple preparations, DeBell soon found himself working beside great chefs such as Michael Chiarello and

> DeBell has lived in Buffalo since the late 1990s, working as executive chef at the Park Lane, Hutch's, Tempo, and Toro.

Daniel Boulud in restaurants in Hawaii, Florence, Venice, and Portofino.

He returned to Colorado to run the esteemed five-star Cucina Rustica in Vail, participating in events like the Epcot Food & Wine Festival and James Beard dinners. DeBell has lived in Buffalo since the late 1990s, working as executive chef at the Park Lane, Hutch's, Tempo, and Toro.

His current position partners his abilities with the esteemed Shatzel family. While working for them, DeBell developed the original, critically acclaimed menu for Buffalo's first gastropub, the Blue Monk, and runs the kitchen at the family's other famous pub, Cole's.

CHALLENGE 11

Heritage Pork

FROM T-MEADOW FARM

VS.

Nickel City Chef
Paul Jenkins
Tempo, Buffalo, NY

Challenging Chef
Jim Guarino
Shango, Buffalo, NY

T-Meadow Farm

Lockport, New York   heritagebreedsusa.com

The unassuming home on Ewings Road in Lockport looks like many others, with a tidy yard, a gravel driveway, and an old weather-scarred barn. What you may not notice, however, are the nearly 100 heritage breed pigs being raised on pasture on the long and narrow T-Meadow Farm property.

Heritage pork was the secret ingredient for Nickel City Chef's eleventh challenge, and part of the reason it was chosen is, well, genetic. The Tamworth and Gloucestershire Old Spot (GOS) hogs being raised by owner Rich Tilyou and his family are genetically similar to their ancestors, and they maintain traits that are no longer found in the new commercial breeds that have been bred to grow fast with the aid of antibiotics and additives, taste mild, have pink meat, and, sadly, have the proper temperament for caged, indoor living.

In 1996, there were only two Gloucestershire Old Spots in the U.S. Since 2004, there have been roughly 200 new registrations, and some consider the Tilyous responsible for the majority of these. In fact, they may be the only farm in the world that has all four color groups of GOS pigs: Red, Green, Blue, and Black. Currently, there are eighty to a hundred pigs on the farm at any given time. Fully a third of the hogs raised by the Tilyous are shipped across the country to be bred, further increasing the GOS and Tamworth populations.

A science teacher by trade, Tilyou actually began this porcine venture with just five heritage hogs in 2005 as a sustainable solution to naturally clearing his property's overgrown pastures. He strategically placed groups of pigs on specific areas of pasture where they cleared trees and roots while also aerating the soil, fertilizing, and decreasing the number of pests. The hogs were then rotated to different pastures, providing them with a fresh variety of food and new land to tame.

But Tamworth and GOS hogs are prized by chefs for their intense pasture-raised flavor and marbling of fat. A well-known farm in downstate New York purchases the majority of Tilyou's young stock, providing the pork to some of the country's best-known chefs and several of New York City's top restaurants. A smaller number are sold directly to local restaurants in Western New York. This is great news, since the most effective way to save a threatened breed of livestock is, quite simply, to eat it.

In 2010, four local restaurants and chefs were regularly buying whole hogs, which they butcher themselves. That number is rapidly growing–faster than the Tilyous can keep up, in fact. This is a testament to the quality of the T-Meadow animals, Tilyous' abilities, and the good farming and business practices to which they adhere.

Heritage pork was the secret ingredient for the eleventh Nickel City Chef challenge, and T-Meadow Farm provided the chefs with ground pork, bacon, and chops. The resulting creations did justice to the efforts of the bold, trendsetting T-Meadow Farm.

Science teacher and farmer, Rich Tilyou is responsible for helping to bring back the endangered Gloucestershire Old Spot hog, a heritage breed prized by chefs.

Nickel City Chef Paul Jenkins of Tempo and his challenger, Chef Jim Guarino of Shango, are both "ingredient driven." This means that quality ingredients are at the forefront when they create a dish. Seasoning and technique are how they showcase an ingredient's positive qualities, rather than the motivation for the development of a dish.

Chef Jenkins does this by sourcing the best ingredients he can lay his hands on, whether they be fresh heirloom tomatoes from Tom Tower's farm in Niagara County or venison from New Zealand. Chef Guarino has a similar style, although as a major player in Buffalo's farm-to-table scene, he feels that the best ingredients are the freshest. Therefore, he purchases as much as he can from local farms year-round. Providing these two chefs with high-quality, heritage pork from Lockport's T-Meadow Farm as the secret ingredient was perfect.

Both chefs remained true to their signature style. Chef Guarino produced comforting, homey dishes injected with the big flavors of New Orleans. The recipe we feature on page 74 is the best dish he served during the competition, a tantalizing spicy pork sausage augmented by truffle oil and a poached duck egg from Painted Meadow Farm. This is similar to an item that appears on his brunch menu, a weekly event for which Shango is well known.

"Although our pork challenge was friendly in nature, there is no question that it was a heated competition. At times the audience was silent with anticipation, at others raucous with excitement."

Nickel City Chef Paul Jenkins' dishes also echoed some of the items found on the menu at Tempo, particularly the second course, his beloved bolognese. Although we didn't know it at the time, this challenge would be Chef Jenkins' last. He retired after the second season to focus on opening a new restaurant.

Although the pork challenge was friendly in nature, there is no question that it was a heated competition. At times the audience was silent with anticipation, at others, raucous with excitement.

Nickel City Chef Jenkins emulsifies a vinaigrette while cameraman Matt Quinn captures the action live, beaming it onto overhead monitors.

73

CHALLENGING CHEF JIM GUARINO'S
Poached Egg and Sausage
with Crawfish over Biscuits

Servings: 4 | Total prep and cooking time: 45 minutes | Preheat oven to 400°F

INGREDIENTS

2 cups flour

1 tablespoon baking powder

1 teaspoon salt

1/4 teaspoon baking soda

1/2 cup unsalted butter, cubed

1 cup buttermilk

2 tablespoons green onions, sliced

1 pound T-Meadow Farm pork, ground

1/2 cup Cheddar cheese, shredded

1 tablespoon minced garlic

2 tablespoons green onion, sliced

1/4 cup fresh sage, chopped

2 teaspoons hot sauce

1 tablespoon Cajun dry spice

Eggs for poaching

1 cup crawfish tail meat

1/4 cup horseradish

2 ounces rice wine vinegar

2 tablespoons orange juice

1 tablespoon truffle oil

4 ounces extra virgin olive oil

DIRECTIONS

Green Onion Biscuit

- Combine dry ingredients in a bowl. Cut in the butter until a crumbly mixture forms. Add the buttermilk and green onion and stir, bringing the dough together quickly and stirring as little as possible to create a light and flaky biscuit. Form into 3-inch circles and bake until golden brown, approximately 15 minutes. Remove and cool on a rack. This step can be done up to 48 hours in advance.

Sausage Patties, Eggs and Crawfish

- Place all ingredients except eggs and crawfish in a bowl and combine thoroughly. Form into patties and set aside.

- Bring water to a boil and begin poaching eggs.

- Set up two hot sauté pans. In one, sear both sides of the sausage until caramelized and cooked through. In the other, sauté the crawfish in butter. Drain the sausage on a paper towel.

Sauce

- Combine the horseradish, vinegar, juice, and truffle oil in a blender. Pulse until combined. Slowly drizzle in the olive oil, creating an emulsion. Set aside.

PLATING

Stack the dish in the following manner: biscuit, sausage, crawfish, egg. Drizzle the sauce. Garnish with chopped green onion or shaved black truffle.

Pasta Bolognese

Nancy J. Parisi

Servings: 8 | Total prep and cooking time: 75 minutes | Preheat oven to 375°F

INGREDIENTS

1 pound lean ground beef

1 pound ground T-Meadow Farm pork butt

1 pound ground veal

1/2 pound pancetta, diced

1 sweet onion, diced finely

4 stalks celery, diced finely

1/2 pound carrots, diced finely

4 cloves elephant garlic, minced

1 liter red table wine

3 14-ounce cans crushed tomatoes, with liquid

1 cup heavy cream

2 tablespoons chopped fresh basil

4 tablespoons chopped fresh flat leaf parsley

Ground nutmeg

Salt and pepper

1 box orecchiette pasta

DIRECTIONS

• Heat a large, heavy-bottomed Dutch oven over medium heat. Add the pancetta, rendering the fat. Once it begins to brown, add the meat and season liberally with salt and freshly ground pepper.

• Continue to cook, stirring with a wooden spoon until the meat is cooked. Add the diced vegetables. Stir to incorporate and cook for about 10 minutes until the onions become translucent. Add the red wine and reduce for 15 minutes.

• Add the tomatoes. Increase the heat and simmer covered for 30 minutes. Remove the lid and slowly add the heavy cream, stirring constantly.

• Once combined, cook for 5 minutes. Season the sauce, to taste, with fresh herbs, nutmeg, salt, and pepper.

• Prepare orecchiette according to package instructions. Do not rinse.

PLATING

Serve on a warm platter over drained (but unrinsed) pasta with freshly grated Parmigiano-Reggiano.

75

CHALLENGING CHEF
Jim Guarino
of Shango

Housemade Pork Sausage on Green Onion Biscuit
Poached Duck Egg, Shaved Truffle, Lemon Oil

Smoked Pork Chop with Chayote Slaw
Hot and Sweet Pickled Peppers, Crawfish, Red Pepper Jelly, and Fried Oyster

Banana Bread Pudding
Bacon Caramel Sauce, Bacon Chocolate Chip Ice Cream

NICKEL CITY CHEF
Paul Jenkins
of Tempo

Bacon-crusted Salmon
Roasted Heirloom Tomatoes, Cauliflower Risotto

Pasta Bolognese
Handmade Gnocchi, Fresh Burrata

Pan-seared Chimichurri Pork Chop
Fried Oyster, Avocado Salad

SCORES FOR CHALLENGE 11

	Challenging Chef Jim Guarino		Nickel City Chef Paul Jenkins
Taste & Flavor	11	Taste & Flavor	11
Creativity	12	Creativity	9
Plating & Presentation	11	Plating & Presentation	12
Technical Execution	9	Technical Execution	11
Use of Secret Ingredient	12	Use of Secret Ingredient	10
Audience Vote	1	Audience Vote	0
Total	**56**		**53**

The Challenger:
Chef Jim Guarino
Shango Bistro and Wine Bar
3260 Main Street, Buffalo
shangobistro.com

Jim Guarino did not set out to be a chef. As owner of one of Buffalo's first and favorite coffeehouses, the Coffee Bean Café, Guarino provided coffee and a hangout for SUNY Buffalo students at his Main Street business through much of the 1990s.

> Chef Guarino's commitment to sustainability pre-dates the trend.

Guarino discovered a love for the city of New Orleans, its cuisine, and the sense of community so deeply entwined in that region's food traditions. He began offering Cajun and Creole-themed dishes at the café, particularly during brunch.

Realizing that this was his next step professionally, Chef Guarino traveled frequently to NOLA and surrounding areas, developing his knowledge and palate. In 2004, he moved forward with his plan for transformation, shuttering the café and reopening a short time later as Shango, a bistro inspired by the flavors of New Orleans.

Shango strives to awaken the senses through its creative menu, a *Wine Spectator*-awarded wine list, and hand-selected beer offerings. Chef Guarino's commitment to sustainability predates the trend and is evidenced in his use of sustainable seafood and the many ingredients he sources from local farms and artisan producers.

CHALLENGE 12

Chicken

FROM GOOD GRASS FARM

 VS.

Nickel City Chef
Krista Van Wagner
Curly's, Lackawanna, NY

Challenging Chef
Mark Sciortino
Marco's, Buffalo, NY

Good Grass Farm

Ashville, New York   goodgrassfarm.com

Yes, the Chautauqua County farmhouse was a bit dilapidated. But Jef Creager and Karen Kearney loved it anyway, and in 1999 the young professional couple took the plunge. They worked diligently to restore it to its former glory, when the farm was a fully functioning dairy.

Concern for their family's health and a love for the earth eventually led them to raise their own food. Today, the couple pasture-raises antibiotic- and hormone-free chickens on their stunning farm in Ashville, New York. Their chickens were an ideal choice as a Nickel City Chef secret ingredient.

Creager and Kearney's interest in healthier, safer chicken mirrors that of much of the country. Over the last few decades, the desire to eat healthful, lean meat has led to a significant increase in demand for poultry and white-meat chicken in particular. An integral part of America's diet, 45 billion chickens are consumed each year.

Yet there is a downside to this growing demand and the subsequent increase in supply. Many chickens are raised confined in cages, fed carefully regulated diets of factory food, and given hormones to speed their growth. In nature, chicks require three months to grow to full size. But using high-tech breeding and hormones, today's factory chickens grow to full size in just forty-five days. In addition, they are bred to have larger breasts, the part most Americans prefer. Due to these practices, the animals are top-heavy and often are unable to stand and support their own weight.

The world of Good Grass Farm is far, far different. Each day the chickens are moved to a new section of rolling pasture, where they spend the morning and afternoon foraging for food, soaking up the sun, and fertilizing the land. Good Grass currently raises Cornish Rock Cross chickens, known for their moist, juicy meat. The animals' varied diet and natural lifestyle create an unparalleled flavor, making this some of the most delicious poultry with which Nickel City Chef has ever had the privilege of working.

In addition to pasture-raised chickens and fresh eggs, Good Grass Farm raises turkeys, cows, pigs, and organic vegetables and berries. Clearly, then, this small family farm is dedicated to taking care of the land it uses and respecting the livestock and produce it raises. The glory days of that dilapidated farmhouse have returned, all thanks to one couple's bold vision.

If nothing else can convince someone of the notable difference in quality that eating locally sourced foods can provide, chicken from Good Grass Farm will do the trick. Jef and Karen's moist, flavorful, and plump chicken can bring chefs and foodies to their knees.

Photos: Good Grass Farm

78

In 2009, I had the pleasure of hosting a farm-to-table dinner in Chautauqua. It was a wonderful night, filled with all the things a perfect dinner party has to offer: like-minded people, delicious food, and ample wine. It was in this setting that I first tasted chicken from Good Grass Farm.

What I am about to tell you may be very revealing about the mind of a diehard foodie, but it's the truth. A handful of well-prepared courses were served to the group, and after a few glasses of wine, excellent discussion ensued. In mid-conversation, the third course appeared and, taking a brief pause, I took a bite.

Any variation of this dish would have been good; a pan-seared chicken breast was served with cauliflower puree, mustard greens, sautéed mushrooms, and a whole grain mustard sauce. It was delicious. But what was truly mind-blowing was the chicken. No, it wasn't the deft seasoning or perfect execution, though those things didn't hurt. This chicken had...flavor. Such flavor that I nearly cried. Really.

"This chicken had...flavor. Such flavor that I nearly cried. Really."

Mid-chew, I realized what that meant about all other chicken I had eaten for nearly four decades. This was an example of how chicken is supposed to taste, and had tasted for centuries prior to the one in which I was born. The flavor came from chickens raised on a green and sunny pasture, that allowed for the natural and varied diet of an animal, rather than a factory farm where animals are confined indoors and fed homogenous feed.

After this experience, naturally I decided to use Good Grass Farm's chicken as a secret ingredient the very next season. The initial impact their chicken had on me in Chautauqua was revisited on the faces of our competing chefs during the challenge as they cooked with it for the first time.

Both participating chefs utilize chicken in their restaurants as the main component of their signature dish. Chef Krista Van Wagner of Curly's is known for her love of Caribbean flavors; some may even say that her career is built on the back of her Jamaican Jerk chicken. Her signature sauce introduced Western New York to the art of jerk seasoning nearly twenty years ago. It is still found on Curly's menu.

Likewise, Chef Mark Sciortino, of the Italian restaurant Marco's, is well-known for his very capable Chicken Parmigiana, a longtime favorite of the restaurant's dedicated clientele.

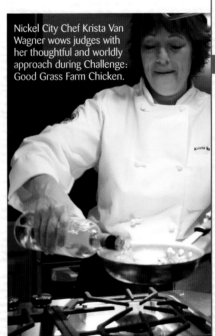

Nickel City Chef Krista Van Wagner wows judges with her thoughtful and worldly approach during Challenge: Good Grass Farm Chicken.

Amazingly, both chefs only nodded at the classic flavor profiles for which each is so well known. Instead, they impressed the audience with unique and flavorful recipes. In the end, Chef Van Wagner's Chicken Française (page 81), along with her third course of chicken schnitzel paired with bone marrow and morel mushrooms, appealed the most to our judges.

First-time-judge Mary Luz Mejia, a Toronto food writer and television producer, was especially impressed. "I thought Mark's dishes were a fun and whimsical take on Italian-American fare. It really showcased his creativity and his roots. He's proud of being Buffalo born and bred, and you can tell. Krista's dishes were very worldly in the sense that she brought in a lot of different European influences...and that chicken schnitzel she made with the thigh was unbelievable. It really highlighted the farmers' passion and the integrity of the product."

CHALLENGING CHEF MARK SCIORTINO'S

Italian Wedding Soup
with Swiss Chard and Chicken Meatballs

Servings: 6 to 8 | Total prep and cooking time: 90 minutes | Preheat oven to 375°F

INGREDIENTS

1 whole 3- to 4-pound Good Grass Farm chicken

2 bunches Swiss chard, washed and dried

1 small onion, diced

2 cloves garlic, minced

2 carrots, diced

1 stalk celery, diced

20 sprigs fresh parsley, washed and chopped

4 tablespoons fennel seed

2 tablespoons crushed red pepper

2 bay leaves

1/2 cup shredded mozzarella

1/2 cup grated Parmesan cheese

1 cup grated Romano cheese

1 box orzo or ditalini

Salt and pepper

Olive oil

DIRECTIONS

• Remove the breast from the chicken and set aside.

• Heat a large pot of water over medium-high heat. Add chicken carcass and bring to a boil.

• Meanwhile, heat a sauté pan over medium heat. Add approximately 2 tablespoons of olive oil. When heated, add half the garlic, and the carrots, celery, and onion to the pan. Cook until soft and translucent.

• Add contents of the pan to the boiling chicken stock. When the chicken is fully cooked, remove from the pot and set aside on a plate or rack to cool. Reduce heat under the stock to low and simmer.

• When cool enough to touch, remove the meat from the chicken carcass and return it to the stock pot. Continue to simmer. Season the stock with salt and pepper to taste. Add bay leaves. Roughly chop the chard and add to the stock.

• Following instructions on the package, cook and strain the pasta. Set aside.

• Remove the skin from the reserved chicken breasts and discard. Using a meat grinder or a food processor, grind the boneless breast. In a medium mixing bowl, thoroughly combine the ground chicken with red pepper, fennel seed, the remaining garlic, Romano, parsley, salt and pepper, and mozzarella. Roll the seasoned meat into small meatballs and place them on a lined baking sheet. Bake for 25 to 30 minutes. Remove from oven and add to stock.

• Check stock for final seasoning. Add salt and pepper to taste.

PLATING

Add a few spoonfuls of pasta to a bowl, topping it with the broth and meatballs. Finish with Parmesan cheese.

Chicken Française
with Crab and Panzanella Salad

Nancy J. Parisi

Servings: 4 | Total prep and cooking time: 1 hour | Preheat oven to 375°F

INGREDIENTS

12 cloves garlic, smashed

1/4 cup olive oil

1 loaf hearty bread, cut in cubes

1/4 red onion, diced

1 pint cherry or grape tomatoes, quartered

Zest of 1 lemon

2 tablespoons capers, chopped

12 large basil leaves, finely chopped

1/2 cup olive oil

1/4 cup balsamic vinegar

---

4 ounces Peekytoe Crab (or any other Maine crab)

4 tablespoons butter

Juice of 1 lemon

1/4 cup white wine

2 teaspoons chopped chives

Salt and pepper

---

4 6-ounce Good Grass Farm chicken breasts, pounded thin

1 egg

1 tablespoon water

2 tablespoons grated Parmesan cheese

1/2 cup flour

1 tablespoon olive oil

6 tablespoons butter

Juice of 1 lemon

1/2 cup white wine

1/4 cup chicken stock

2 tablespoons chopped parsley

Salt and pepper

DIRECTIONS

Panzanella Salad

• Put garlic in a sauté pan. Add olive oil and bring to simmer. Allow to cool. Strain, reserving the oil and discarding the garlic.

• Toss bread cubes with garlic oil and toast in oven until golden brown and crispy. Combine olive oil and vinegar and set aside. In a large mixing bowl add the onions, cherry tomatoes, lemon zest, capers, and basil.

• Add bread and reserved oil-and-vinegar mixture. Toss. Season with salt and pepper to taste. Let stand while completing the rest of the dish.

Lemon Crab

• Brown butter in a sauté pan. Add wine and lemon juice and bring to a boil. Add crab. Simmer until warmed through. Remove from pan and finish with salt, pepper, and chives.

Chicken Française

• Whip eggs, water, and cheese together. Season the breasts with salt and pepper. Dredge in flour, then coat in egg mixture. Heat a sauté pan over medium heat. Add 2 tablespoons of the butter and the olive oil. Sear the chicken, browning on both sides. When cooked through, remove from pan and set aside.

• Discard the butter-and-oil mixture. Deglaze the pan with white wine. Lower the heat to medium. Add lemon juice and reduce the liquid by half. Finish the sauce with the remaining butter. Mix gently. Do not boil or this sauce will break. Finish with salt, pepper, and fresh parsley.

PLATING

Place Panzanella salad on plate, top with crab meat and sliced chicken breast. Finish with lemon butter sauce and garnish with fresh basil.

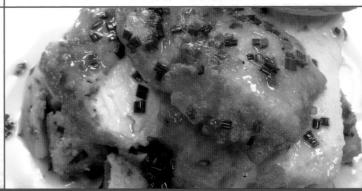

81

CHALLENGING CHEF
Mark Sciortino
of Marco's

Italian Wedding Soup
with Chicken Meatballs

Chicken Cacciatore

Buffalo-style Chicken Gnocchi

NICKEL CITY CHEF
Krista Van Wagner
of Curly's

Frisée Salad
Jerk Chicken Foot, Mango Salsa,
Pickled Onion

Chicken Française
Panzanella Salad, Peekytoe
Crab, Scape, Basil Oil

Chicken Schnitzel
Bone Marrow, Sweet Pea and
Morel Cream Sauce,
Fried Morel

SCORES FOR CHALLENGE 12

	Challenging Chef Mark Sciortino	Nickel City Chef Krista Van Wagner	
Taste & Flavor	11	Taste & Flavor	11
Creativity	10	Creativity	11
Plating & Presentation	10	Plating & Presentation	12
Technical Execution	11	Technical Execution	12
Use of Secret Ingredient	11	Use of Secret Ingredient	11
Audience Vote	1	Audience Vote	0
Total	**54**		**57**

82

The Challenger:
Chef Mark Sciortino

Marco's Fine Italian Dining
1085 Niagara Street, Buffalo
marcosbuffalo.com

Chef Mark Sciortino opened Marco's on
Niagara Street in 1988, serving dishes that
quickly became family favorites. In 1998 he
opened Marco's Italian Deli
on Hertel, and another Western New
York favorite was born. The buzz
continued to build and Marco's Deli
continued to grow, this time by

> Sciortino attributes his success to the help and support of his family, friends, and customers.

franchising. Two more locations opened in Kenmore
and Williamsville.

In 2008, Buffalo-based Sorrento® Cheese
hired Sciortino as its spokesperson. This led to
appearances on national television shows and live
cooking demonstrations at Italian festivals across
the country. A strong proponent of Buffalo and its
restaurant scene, Sciortino volunteers his time to
various events and fundraisers in the community on a regular
basis. The busy chef and his wife, Victoria, are the proud
parents of twin girls, Maria and Gabriella. In typical Buffalo
fashion, Sciortino attributes his success to the help and
support of his family, friends, and customers.

CHALLENGE 13

Apples

FROM DAN TOWER FARM

 VS.

Nickel City Chef
Krista Van Wagner
Curly's, Lackawanna, NY

Challenging Chef
Jennifer Boye
The Mansion on Delaware
Avenue, Buffalo, NY

Dan Tower Farm

Youngstown, New York   dantowerfarm.com

When the four generations that came before you were farmers, you are probably destined to work the fields yourself. This was the case with Dan Tower, who currently operates Dan Tower Farm along the Niagara Escarpment. Best known for its thirty varieties of apples— a Nickel City Chef secret ingredient—and custom-pressed cider, this family-operated farm also raises cherries, plums, peaches, strawberries, and raspberries.

Dan and his wife, Iris, believe in allowing Mother Nature to do her job. To that end, they use natural methods as often as possible to maintain their fields. In the spring, beehives are placed throughout the orchards to encourage pollination. Mowing helps with weed control, and farm-friendly insects, such as praying mantises and ladybugs, are gladly seen. Tower is careful to take weather reports into consideration before plowing, planting, pruning, or spraying for worms, pests, and weeds. He also uses what he considers a "low spray" schedule to keep his produce flourishing at optimal levels without using higher applications of unnecessary chemicals.

Apples have always kept well into winter, but the Towers use an atmosphere-controlled system to keep their apples fresh, crisp, and delicious well into the season. This process is what allowed Nickel City Chef to use Dan Tower apples as the secret ingredient for its thirteenth competition in the chilly month of February. The chefs had the option of using two varieties: Idareds and Crispins.

Idared apples were released commercially in 1942 and are best known for their beautiful red and green skin and ability to survive long periods of storage. They are tart and juicy, which makes them great for cooking. The Crispin apple has its roots in Japan, where it is known as a Mutsu. Its speckled green skin may make one think

of a Granny Smith apple, but Crispins are sweet, refreshing, and very crisp. They are excellent sliced raw in salads or baked into pie.

New York State is the second largest apple-growing state in the country (Washington State leads), producing more than twenty-five million bushels each year. The state's favorable soil, rainfall, and temperatures are especially conducive to apple growing. Sadly, studies show that most fresh apples eaten in New York City do not come from New York State.

As the importance of buying locally becomes increasingly clear, buying apples–long considered America's favorite fruit–is an easy way for every consumer to make a choice that benefits New York State's local economy. One bite of a Dan Tower Farm apple seals the deal.

Dan and Iris Tower raise a large variety of fruit on their Niagara County farm. In 2011 they added a membership-based Community Supported Agriculture (CSA) option for their customers.

Men have dominated the professional cooking industry for decades, and Western New York is no exception. For the first competition in season three, Nickel City Chef was proud to offer our audience the chance to see a challenge featuring two of Buffalo's best chefs, both of whom are women.

The crowd's enthusiasm was contagious, which helped stave off any nervousness that might have been felt by our staff or the competing chefs. In one kitchen was Chef Jennifer Boye of The Mansion on Delaware Avenue. In the other was Nickel City Chef Krista Van Wagner, who had just come off a season of wins. She is known for her good sportsmanship, but I also know she wanted to win!

Our secret ingredient was apples, an important crop in New York State, and a fruit that stores well for consumption in cold weather. "When I saw the apples," says Boye, "I thought, 'The possibilities are endless.'"

In the past, challengers have struggled to keep up with the long-practiced team of Krista Van Wagner and her husband, Kirk. After going to culinary school and traveling the world together, they took over Krista's grandfather's restaurant where they cook side-by-side. They know each other's moves, thoughts, and style, and work together like a well-oiled machine.

Boye and her sous chef, Jamie Zynda, had worked together for only a short time, but they were no less impressive. Their kitchen remained neat and organized, and they communicated effortlessly throughout the event, all while under tremendous pressure. Senior chefs in the audience commented on this after the show, including our cohost, chef Mike Andrzejewski of Seabar. He noted not only their teamwork, but their overall ability to successfully execute a menu using solid technique.

Both chefs created beautiful plates filled with color and texture. While every dish was strong, the dessert course especially highlighted the secret ingredient. Van Wagner's apple cake with caramel sauce and high-quality goat cheese was perfectly portioned and the contrast of flavors resulting from the pairing of the cheese and apples was very satisfying.

"The Boye/Zynda kitchen remained neat and organized, and they communicated effortlessly throughout the event, all while under tremendous pressure. Senior chefs in the audience commented on this after the show, including our cohost, Chef Mike Andrzejewski"

Anna L. Miller

Nickel City Chef Van Wagner impresses the judges with her successful use of apples in savory dishes. The saffron-saturated apples served with her second course drew raves.

Boye's "Apple Study" was equally delicious, though less about contrasts and more about technique. Her apple eggnog tasted wonderfully fresh, and the use of cheddar in the crust of the apple crisp was a great play on classic Americana.

It was a very close score and tough decision for our panel of judges, which included Mary Luz Mejia, a Canadian food writer and television producer who had also visited us the previous year for our chicken challenge. "What I love about Krista's food is that she puts the world on a plate," she told us after the show. "You can taste the Caribbean, you can taste her time in Europe. Krista brings her A-game when it comes to spicing, flavor, and texture."

Season three was also the first time Nickel City Chef offered the general public a chance to purchase season tickets, and the audience was packed with fans of the event, many of whom had not missed a single battle. Challenge 13: Apples from Dan Tower Farm was full of excitement and anticipation, and the food prepared exhibited excellent technique and decision-making by both chefs.

Apple Sauerkraut Pierogi
with Apple Beer-braised Onions and Caraway Crème Fraîche

Servings: 4 | Total prep and cooking time: 1 hour (not including fermentation)

INGREDIENTS

1 cup heavy whipping cream

2 tablespoons buttermilk

1 teaspoon lemon juice

1 tablespoon caraway seeds

Salt and pepper

---

2 medium Dan Tower Farm Idared apples, peeled and diced

8 slices double smoked bacon, diced

1 medium sweet onion, diced

1 14-ounce can sauerkraut, drained

1 small clove garlic, minced

Salt and pepper

---

2 1/2 to 3 cups all-purpose flour

2 teaspoons kosher salt

1 large egg

3 tablespoons sour cream

1/2 cup tepid water

---

2 Dan Tower Farm Crispin apples, thinly sliced

1 medium sweet onion, thinly sliced

2 tablespoons butter

1/2 cup apple lambic beer

Salt and pepper

DIRECTIONS

Crème Fraîche

• Combine cream, buttermilk, and lemon juice in a glass bowl. Cover and let stand at room temperature for 24 to 36 hours until very thick. Stir well and refrigerate. Stir in salt, pepper, and caraway seeds right before serving.

Apple Sauerkraut Filling

• Fry bacon in a large sauté pan. Remove and set aside, leaving bacon grease in pan. Add apples and onions to pan and sauté until soft. Add garlic, sauerkraut, and reserved bacon to pan and sauté over medium heat until mixture is heated through and thoroughly combined. Season with salt and pepper and set aside.

Pierogi Dough

• In a large bowl, mix all ingredients together and knead for just a few moments. Dough will look a bit lumpy, and it should be quite sticky. Cover dough and let sit for about 30 minutes. Take a portion of the dough and, on a floured surface, roll very thin (about 1/16 inches thick). To prevent sticking, you will need plenty of flour as you roll. Cut circles of dough with a medium-sized round cutter or the top of a water glass. Place a small amount of sauerkraut filling in the middle of each circle. Brush a small amount of water on the edge of each circle and fold in half. Press edges together, sealing the filling and creating a half-moon. Repeat process until dough and filling are gone. Bring a large pot of liberally salted water to a boil and drop in pierogi, a few at a time. Boil pierogi for 3 to 4 minutes, until they float and puff a bit. Drain, place on a greased cookie sheet in a single layer, and set aside.

Apple Beer-braised Onions

• Melt butter in a medium sauté pan and add apples and onions. Sauté until semisoft. Add beer, salt, and pepper and cook until most of the beer has evaporated.

PLATING

Sauté pierogi in a good amount of melted butter until golden brown and heated through. Place a small pile of the warmed apple-onion mixture in the middle of a serving dish. Place two pierogi on top of the mixture. Top pierogi with a dollop of caraway crème fraîche and garnish with a sprig of fresh dill or some grated beetroot.

86

Apple Cake
with Chutney and Goat Cheese

Nancy J. Parisi

Servings: 8 | Total prep and cooking time: 75 minutes | Preheat oven to 350°F

INGREDIENTS

3 cups all-purpose flour

3 cups Dan Tower Farm Idared apples, peeled and chopped

1 teaspoon baking soda

1 teaspoon cinnamon

1/4 teaspoon salt

3 eggs

1 1/2 cups vegetable oil

2 cups sugar

2 teaspoons vanilla extract

1 cup walnuts, chopped

1 cup brown sugar

1/4 cup milk

1/2 cup unsalted butter, cubed

---

2 tablespoons unsalted butter

1/2 teaspoon minced fresh ginger

2 tablespoons brown sugar

2 tablespoons rice wine vinegar

2 Dan Tower Farm Crispin apples, peeled and diced

2 Dan Tower Farm Idared apples, peeled and diced

3 tablespoons dried cherries

1 cinnamon stick

PLATING

Arrange small portions of chutney and apple cake with a wedge of good, ash-ripened goat cheese. Krista recommends Bonne Bouche. Caramel sauce is an excellent way to dress up this sophisticated dessert.

DIRECTIONS

Apple Cake

• In a mixing bowl, sift together flour, soda, cinnamon, and salt. In a separate bowl, beat eggs, oil, and sugar for 3 minutes at high speed. Slowly add the dry ingredients, mixing to combine. Stir in vanilla. Gently fold in apples and nuts. Pour into a greased and floured 9 by 13-inch pan. Bake for 50 minutes. Just before removing cake from the oven, mix the brown sugar, butter, and milk in a sauce pan on the stove. Bring to a boil over medium heat and stir constantly until the sugar is completely dissolved. Remove the cake from oven and pour the brown sugar mixture over the cake. Set aside to cool.

Apple Chutney

• In a small saucepan over medium heat, melt the butter until golden brown. Add ginger and brown sugar. Stir until the sugar is completely dissolved. Add the apples, cinnamon stick, rice wine vinegar, and dried cherries. Simmer 10 minutes. Cool.

87

CHALLENGING CHEF
Jennifer Boye
of The Mansion on Delaware Avenue

Apples Three Ways:
- Celeriac Crispin Soup
- Idared Sauerkraut Pierogi,
  Apple Beer-braised Onions,
  Caraway Crème Fraîche
- Arugula Salad of Apples, Manchego,
  Pomegranate, Apple-Rosemary
  Vinaigrette

Bacon-wrapped Antelope Leg
Crispy Apple Potato Pancake,
Apple Bacon Marmalade

Apple, Green Tomato Crisp
with Cheddar Streusel
Apple Eggnog with Cinnamon
Mascarpone, Toffee Apple Truffles

NICKEL CITY CHEF
Krista Van Wagner
of Curly's

Pan-seared Skatewing
Chive Beurre Blanc, Saffron-poached
Apple Slaw

Wild Arkansas Mallard Duck Breast
Calvados, Cider Beurre Noisette,
Apple Foie Gras Hash

Apple Cake
Bonne Bouche of Ash-ripened Goat
Cheese, Ginger Apple Chutney,
Caramel Sauce

SCORES FOR CHALLENGE 13

	Challenging Chef Jennifer Boye		Nickel City Chef Krista Van Wagner
Taste & Flavor	12	Taste & Flavor	12
Creativity	10	Creativity	11
Plating & Presentation	12	Plating & Presentation	11
Technical Execution	11	Technical Execution	11
Use of Secret Ingredient	9	Use of Secret Ingredient	11
Audience Vote	1	Audience Vote	0
Total	**55**		**56**

88

The Challenger:
Jennifer Boye
Mansion on Delaware Avenue
414 Delaware Avenue, Buffalo
mansionondelaware.com

Born and raised in Buffalo, Boye knew at an early age that cooking in a professional setting was in her future. She comes from a family of talented cooks and food lovers, and virtually every family gathering was a culinary event.

Boye attended the culinary program at Erie Community College, and after graduation her cooking career officially began at the Transit Valley Country Club. There she was able to practice the art of cooking and baking for large groups. After almost four

With chef Boye installed in the kitchen, tending the seasonal garden, and preparing fabulous meals ...the small hotel has secured a position as one of the most elegant and delicious ways to enjoy Buffalo.

years as executive chef at the much-loved Fiddleheads restaurant in Allentown, she moved on to fill the same position at The Mansion on Delaware Avenue (MoDA).

At the time, MoDA was a newly restored example of Buffalo's amazing architecture. A decade later it is a treasure, lauded by AAA, Zagat, Conde Nast, and Arthur Frommer. With chef Boye installed in the kitchen, tending the seasonal garden, and preparing fabulous meals for those who book events at the small hotel, MoDA has secured a position as one of the most elegant and delicious ways to enjoy Buffalo.

Anna L. Miller

CHALLENGE 14

Tomatoes

FROM H2GRO

 VS.

Nickel City Chef
Brian Mietus
Bacchus, Buffalo, NY

Challenging Chef
Mary Ann Giordano
Creekview Restaurant,
Williamsville, NY

H2Gro
Lewiston, NY   h2gro.net

Lewiston's H2Gro is a state-of-the-art 12.5-acre hydroponic greenhouse facility, and a pretty darned cool one. A fascinating example of advancement in environmentally sound greenhouses, it has been recognized by the Planet Green Channel and others for its amazing ability to convert methane from a local landfill into energy. This energy, in turn, powers eleven engines that produce the electricity required to run the H2Gro greenhouses and hydroponics.

Thanks to this process, fresh, vine-ripened tomatoes are available to Western New Yorkers during the winter months. Their choice as a Nickel City Chef secret ingredient led to an unforgettable challenge.

While many industrial tomato-growing facilities use chemical enhancers to grow bigger tomatoes at a faster rate, H2Gro's vine-ripened tomatoes are allowed to ripen naturally. Even with this longer (or, perhaps more accurately, not prematurely shortened) growing time, H2Gro harvests 15,000 pounds of tomatoes per day. And while the growing season is somewhat limited by weather constraints, H2Gro is still able to produce 6 million pounds of tomatoes per year. This includes picking and packing on a daily basis for more than 100 area outlets.

The facility is pesticide free and uses Integrated Pest Management to maintain balance. In addition, the water used for irrigation is recycled and reused. Hydroponic growing entails no soil, but a neutral growing medium. H2Gro uses crushed coconut husk in a bag into which the young plants are placed and fed nutrients.

This facility is managed by Eric Toye, general manager. He says, "For H2Gro to be successful, it is very important to have local support." Happily, H2Gro's local support is growing as quickly as its tomatoes. H2Gro has experienced a roughly 50 percent increase in the volume of tomatoes sold in the community versus the volume shipped elsewhere.

Being able to eat local tomatoes nearly year-round is a real treat, and the competitors in the Nickel City Chef fourteenth challenge used them in a variety of creative ways. Fortunately for Western New Yorkers, H2Gro's sustainably raised tomatoes are fresh off the vine and in local supermarkets March through December each year.

This competition was the first in which Brian Mietus participated as a Nickel City Chef, replacing Tempo's Paul Jenkins after his retirement from the series. Since Mietus won the first-ever Nickel City Chef competition (Challenge: Eggs) in season one, loves to compete, and has been the managing partner of the highly successful Bacchus restaurant for several years, he was eminently qualified for the job and became an enthusiastic member of the team.

Interestingly, he and challenging chef Mary Ann Giordano had competed in a culinary competition before, with Giordano emerging the winner. For those who closely follow such things, this may have seemed like a rematch. I, however, was unaware of that fact when we were determining the best matches for season three. Fortunately, with their excellent attitude and love of competition, there were no grudges or hurt feelings.

> *"Mietus took technical risks. You could see chefs in the audience shaking their heads in disbelief when it was announced that Mietus intended to make a consommé in less than an hour."*

Unlike many of the other challenges in which produce was the secret ingredient, Challenge: Tomatoes featured only one variety: red, vine-ripened tomatoes. The chefs were allowed to incorporate other types of tomatoes and tomato products in their dishes, but H2Gro's vine-ripened tomatoes had to be used in each dish.

Chef Mietus chose a simple and classic approach with his menu. Chef Giordano, whose Creekview Restaurant offers standard American fare and a handful of European and Latin American dishes, chose a menu inspired by her presonal passion for Mediterranean flavors.

Mietus took technical risks. You could see chefs in the audience shaking their heads in disbelief when it was announced that Mietus intended to make a consommé in less than an hour. Mietus knew it was a risk, but he was also excited about trying a new method which accelerates the cooking process.

"Brian's approach was very refined," commented one of the day's judges, chef Matthew Mytro from Cleveland's restaurant, Crisp. "He has worked in a number of great places and that showed in his cooking. He used some very difficult techniques, like the clarification process for making consommé. That's something where you typically need two hours of prep time." Unfortunately, the judges felt that the tomato flavor didn't come through in several of his courses, including the consommé.

Giordano had a few issues, too. The judges felt she could have made the tomatoes more of a focus in each dish, but they appreciated how colorful her dishes were and loved the spices she used to heighten and enhance the tomatoes' overall flavor.

Nickel City Chef Mietus prepares tomatoes for his Tomato Tart (page 93), a careful play between savory and sweet which uses techniques typically reserved for the classic French dessert, Tarte Tatin.

kc kratt

CHALLENGING CHEF MARY ANN GIORDANO'S

Grilled Lamb Romesco
with Farro Salad

Servings: 4 | Total prep and cooking time: 90 minutes | Preheat grill

INGREDIENTS

1 16 to 20 ounce boneless loin of lamb

2 tablespoons fennel seeds

2 tablespoons fresh rosemary

2 tablespoons kosher salt

1 tablespoon black pepper

---

4 H2Gro tomatoes, chopped

2 roasted red peppers, chopped

1/2 cup diced onion

1/2 cup toasted almonds

1 teaspoon red wine vinegar

1/2 cup fresh basil

1/2 cup fresh mint

1 teaspoon chopped garlic

2 tablespoons smoked paprika (pimenton)

1 cup olive oil

1 slice Italian bread, grilled or toasted

---

6 cups water

2 cups farro

1 teaspoon kosher salt

2 pounds fresh fava beans

1 cup Feta cheese, shredded or crumbled

1 cup toasted walnuts

I cup fresh basil

1/2 cup fresh lemon juice

1 cup olive oil

DIRECTIONS

Lamb

• Trim any silver skin from the loin, but leave the fat cap intact for flavor. Heat a nonstick sauté pan over medium heat. Add the fennel, stirring continuously so as not to burn. Once the seeds have become fragrant, remove to a cutting board. Rub the lamb with salt. Roughly chop the rosemary and combine with salt and pepper. Rub lamb with the spice mixture. Set aside, allowing the lamb to come to room temperature.

• Grill lamb fat side down on a hot grill. Char well on both sides but try to avoid large flames. Lamb should cook 5 to 7 minutes on each side, until medium rare. Allow lamb to rest for 10 minutes before slicing.

Romesco Sauce

• In a sauté pan over medium heat, cook the onions, peppers, and tomatoes until the onions are translucent. Add the garlic and paprika. In a blender combine with remaining ingredients and purée. Romesco sauce can be served room temperature or hot.

Farro Salad

• In a large Dutch oven combine water, farro, salt, and a drizzle of olive oil. Bring to a boil. Reduce heat and simmer until water is absorbed, approximately 20 minutes.

• Remove the fava beans from their pods. Bring a second pot of salted water to a boil. Add the fava beans and cook for 5 minutes. Cool and slip off the fava beans' second skin. Combine all ingredients. Serve at room temperature.

PLATING

You may stuff fresh H2Gro tomatoes with this salad by hollowing them out and filling them with the mixture. Then drizzle them with olive oil and bake them in a 350°F oven for 15 minutes. Or, you may wish to fill a platter with the salad and serve the slices of lamb loin on top, family-style. Spoon the Romesco sauce over the lamb before serving.

Nancy J. Parisi

NICKEL CITY CHEF BRIAN MIETUS'
Tomato Tart

Servings: 4 | Total prep and cooking time: 1 hour | Preheat oven to 425°F

INGREDIENTS

1 1/3 cups all-purpose flour

1/2 teaspoon salt

1/2 cup cold unsalted butter, cubed

1/4 cup ice water, as needed

8 ripe H2Gro tomatoes

8 ounces mascarpone

4 tablespoons fresh basil, chiffonade

1/8 cup balsamic vinegar

8 tablespoons candied ginger, minced

8 tablespoons confectioner's sugar

Nonstick pan spray

1 egg

DIRECTIONS

• Combine flour and salt in a food processor by pulsing. Add the butter a few cubes at a time, pulsing 6 to 8 times, until the flour resembles coarse meal. Add ice water 1 tablespoon at a time, pulsing until the mixture just begins to clump together.

• Remove dough from machine and place in a mound on a clean surface. Gently shape into a disc. Do not over-knead. Wrap the disc in plastic wrap and refrigerate for at least 1 hour.

• Remove the dough from the refrigerator and allow to sit at room temperature for 5 to 10 minutes. Lightly flour work surface and use a rolling pin to roll out the dough. When it is about 1/8-inch thick, cut the dough to fit your tart pans. Set aside.

• Bring a large pot of water to boil. Prepare an ice bath. Core the tomatoes. Score the skin by using a knife to make an "x" on the bottom. Using tongs, dip the tomatoes into the boiling water. When the skin begins to curl (approximately 15 to 20 seconds), remove the tomatoes to the ice bath. Cool slightly. Cut the tomatoes into quarters and remove the seeds. Pat the pieces dry with a paper towel. Spray tart shells lightly with nonstick pan spray. Coat each pan with sugar. Lay the tomatoes side-by side, covering as much of the pan's surface as possible.

• In a mixing bowl, whisk the mascarpone with the ginger, basil and powdered sugar. Place a small dollop of the cream in the center of the tomato tart.

• Cover the tarts with pie dough. In a small bowl, beat egg with 1 tablespoon of water. Brush the pastry dough with egg wash. Bake for 30 minutes at 425°F, or until the pie dough is golden brown. Serve with a drizzle of balsamic vinegar.

Chef's notes

To chiffonade basil, stack leaves, roll and thinly slice with a sharp knife to create fine, thin strips.

93

CHALLENGING CHEF
Mary Ann Giordano
of Creekview Restaurant

Panzanella Salad
Goat Cheese, White Balsamic
Golden Tomato Vinaigrette

Blue Corn Seafood Enchiladas
Red Chili Tomato Cream,
Salsa, Avocado Lime Purée

Grass-fed Colorado Lamb
Romesco
Eggplant Tomato Purse,
Stuffed Tomato

NICKEL CITY CHEF
Brian Mietus
of Bacchus

Tomato Camembert Sandwich
Tomato Consommé

Bacon-wrapped Monkfish
Basil Risotto, Lobster, Avocado,
Tomato Confit, Tomato
Vinaigrette

Tomato Tart Tatin
Ginger Mascarpone Cream,
Balsamic Reduction

SCORES FOR CHALLENGE 14

	Challenging Chef Mary Ann Giordano		Nickel City Chef Brian Mietus
Taste & Flavor	9	Taste & Flavor	6
Creativity	9	Creativity	9
Plating & Presentation	11	Plating & Presentation	9
Technical Execution	8	Technical Execution	7
Use of Secret Ingredient	9	Use of Secret Ingredient	6
Audience Vote	1	Audience Vote	0
Total	**47**		**37**

The Challenger:
Mary Ann Giordano
Creekview Restaurant
5329 Main Street, Williamsville
creekviewrestaurant.com

Chef Mary Ann Giordano describes her cuisine as "American Fusion," drawing from Mediterranean, Italian, European, and Asian influences. With a degree in science and more than twenty-five years of experience in the restaurant industry, Giordano has been the executive chef at Williamsville's Creekview Restaurant since 1997. Her naturally competitive nature has led her to participate in a variety of culinary competitions throughout her career.

Chef Giordano notes that her memories of childhood include being "surrounded by food and life in the kitchen." Those memories played a major role in the choices she has made in her professional life. Not only does Giordano cook from the heart, but the passion she and her father share for the traditional St. Joseph's Day feast, a Sicilian tradition, has her hard at work on a cookbook featuring her take on that holiday's traditional recipes.

> Her naturally competitive nature has led her to participate in a variety of culinary competitions throughout her career.

Beer

FROM FLYING BISON

VS.

95

Nickel City Chef
JJ Richert
Torches, Buffalo, NY

Challenging Chef
James D. Roberts
Park Country Club,
Williamsville, NY

Flying Bison

Buffalo, NY   flyingbisonbrewing.com

It's no secret that Buffalonians love their beer. The tradition of brewing in this area dates back much further than many people realize. Joseph Webb opened the city's first microbrewery in 1811. Unfortunately, that brewery was burned down by the British during the War of 1812, but neither fire nor warfare could keep the suds from flowing. By 1875, Buffalo was home to more than thirty-eight breweries, and in 1908 alone, local breweries produced more than thirty-one million gallons of beer. In 2005, a study found that 50 percent of Buffalonians had consumed at least one beer in the past thirty days, ranking the city fourth in the nation for per capita beer consumption.

It was only a matter of time, then, before beer was picked as a Nickel City Chef secret ingredient, and the brewer chosen was Flying Bison Brewing Company, located on Ontario Street on Buffalo's West Side. Interestingly, it is the first stand-alone brewery to operate within the City of Buffalo since Iroquois Brewing closed its doors in 1972.

Founder Tim Herzog's personal commitment to fostering the return of brewing to Buffalo is what has carried the brewery through change and rough times. In 2010, Flying Bison struck a deal with Utica, New York-based F. X. Matt Brewing Company in an effort to refine and improve its distribution process. In addition to a commitment to brewing, Flying Bison also has an impressive record of community involvement. It is nearly impossible to attend a local charity event without bumping into a keg of fresh Flying Bison beer. Herzog and Flying Bison are also founders of Buffalo's wildly popular Beerfest, which takes place every August and benefits the Buffalo Hearing and Speech Center.

Good beer made by good people—what more can there be to this story? Well, a more complete description of the beer is certainly in order. Flying Bison's Blackbird Oatmeal Stout and Belgian Dubbel are the two seasonal brews that were featured in the Nickel City Chef fifteenth challenge. The Oatmeal Stout has an ebony color with ruby highlights and a full malt nose with hints of coffee and dark chocolate. Its flavor starts as a dense, bready malt experience, but the pinch of English hops and the espresso character from the roasted barley prevent any syrupy feel. The addition of oats gives this stout a silky finish that is drinkable on its own or when paired with food.

The Belgian Dubbel beer made by Flying Bison features a red color and firm base of malt. The use of Belgian yeast adds another dimension, and the beer has noticeable clove, hints of fruit, and an overall yeasty flavor that further enhance its dimension.

For those looking to pick up a six-pack of Flying Bison, there are several area stores where the brewery's Aviator Red and Buffalo Lager can be found. But a visit to the brewery is a real treat and can be arranged by phoning ahead. It provides a first-hand view of a revived Western New York tradition.

Tim Herzog is founder and operator of Flying Bison Brewery, the first stand-alone brewery to operate in the City of Buffalo since 1972.

O f all the shows, this competition seems to be the one that people want to discuss the most. Is it because the secret ingredient was beer, a beverage near and dear to the hearts of Buffalonians? Is it the fanciful display of artistry exhibited by both chefs during competition? Could the very close final scores be a factor? I don't know, but it was a great example of just how much fun a Nickel City Chef competition can be for audience and competitors alike.

Cooking with beer is fun, but it isn't easy. Improper handling can ruin a meal. I had planned to use Flying Bison beer as a secret ingredient since the series began in 2009, but I wanted to be sure that we scheduled chefs who had a basic understanding of beer's sometimes tempestuous nature. Once the schedule for season three was in place, I knew that pitting Nickel City Chef JJ Richert against Park Country Club's executive chef James Roberts presented the perfect opportunity. These chefs are not just familiar with beer and its use in culinary applications, they are also both passionate consumers.

"These chefs are not just familiar with beer and its use in culinary applications, they are also both passionate consumers."

Neither chef disappointed. Not only did each offer a menu representative of their personality and cooking style, but both went out of their way to ensure that the packed house had a bit of an adventure. Chef Richert used power tools to carve ice mugs on set, brandishing them with the initials of the judges. Chef Roberts created two amazing nitrogen ice creams, each featuring one of the beers provided by Flying Bison. As if the display of preparing nitrogen-cooled ice cream made of stout and Dubbel weren't enough, he won "oohs" and "ahhs" by topping this sundae with bourbon-infused maraschino cherries.

The audience was electric with excitement, and the energy in the Artisan Kitchens & Baths showroom was palpable. Some of the audience may have caught on to the secret ingredient early, as it was hard not to notice the tall, handlebar-mustachioed man known throughout the city for his liquid contributions. Fortunately for us, Flying Bison's Tim Herzog is not just a talented and dedicated microbrewer, but also a well-traveled foodie and a skilled home cook. You may wonder why that would matter, but it really did.

A national television personality with a well-documented love of beer was slated to join our panel of judges, which included Ivy Knight, a Canadian food writer and chef, and comedienne Kristen Becker. Due to a scheduling conflict, the national judge was unable to attend, but our staff was expecting him right up until the moment the audience arrived, just forty-five minutes before the competition was scheduled to begin. When it appeared that he would not be coming, we scrambled to find a last-minute replacement.

At this point we did something we swore we wouldn't do after the lessons learned in the first season: We asked the artisan behind the secret ingredient to be a judge. Tim Herzog took his new role as judge very seriously and, along with the rest of the room, watched as these two talented chefs prepared a dizzying selection of dishes using beer. When it came time to taste the food and offer commentary, Herzog proved to be one of the most articulate and knowledgeable judges we've ever had, weighing in with both praise and criticism.

In the end, it was a close call. Both chefs exhibited great passion for the ingredient, and each used his own style to create unique and sometimes even exhilarating examples of how beer can be used as an ingredient. With only a single point marking the difference between winner and loser, challenging Chef Roberts defeated the previously undefeated Nickel City Chef Richert. Despite the disappointment I am sure that Chef Richert felt at losing, this competition ended in true Nickel City Chef fashion, with a sense of community and pride in the level of culinary skill present in Western New York.

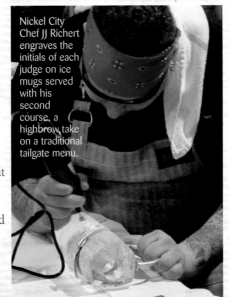
Nickel City Chef JJ Richert engraves the initials of each judge on ice mugs served with his second course, a highbrow take on a traditional tailgate menu.

97

James D. Roberts

CHALLENGING CHEF JAMES D. ROBERT'S

Belgian Onion Soup
with Cave-aged Gruyère

Servings: 4 | Total prep and cooking time: 45 minutes | Preheat broiler

INGREDIENTS

1 teaspoon extra virgin olive oil

1 Spanish onion, julienned

5 shallots, sliced

1 teaspoon fresh thyme

1/2 teaspoon crushed red pepper

1 teaspoon minced garlic

1 1/2 cups Flying Bison Belgian Dubbel beer

1 tablespoon unsalted butter

4 slices sourdough bread, toasted

1 cup shredded Cave-aged Gruyère

1 scallion, sliced

DIRECTIONS

• Heat a heavy-bottomed soup pot over medium heat. Add the olive oil, onion, shallots, thyme, red pepper, and garlic, cooking until translucent. Deglaze the pan with beer. Add the butter and bring to a boil. Reduce heat and simmer for 10 to 15 minutes.

• When ready to serve, turn on the broiler. Ladle the soup into ovenproof crocks. Top each crock with the bread and 1/4 cup of the cheese. Heat under broiler for just a few minutes, until cheese is thoroughly melted and begins to brown on the edges. Garnish with sliced scallion.

98

NICKEL CITY CHEF JJ RICHERT'S
Chocolate Stout Pie

Nancy J. Parisi

Servings: 8 | Total prep and cooking time: 90 minutes | Preheat oven to 375°F

INGREDIENTS

1 1/2 cups all-purpose flour

3/4 cup unsalted butter, cubed

1 teaspoon salt

3 tablespoons sugar

4 tablespoons cream cheese

2 tablespoons cold water, more or less

DIRECTIONS

Crust

- In a large mixing bowl, combine flour, salt, and sugar. Cut in butter and combine until mixture resembles coarse meal. Cut in cream cheese. Sprinkle cold water over this mixture gradually, and mix just until the dough holds together, being careful not to overwork.

- Gather the dough into a disc, wrap in plastic wrap, and refrigerate for at least 30 minutes. Gently turn it out onto a floured board and roll to about a 1/4-inch thick circle large enough to fill a greased pie pan. Set in cooler until filling is prepared.

3 eggs

1 cup light brown sugar

1 teaspoon vanilla extract

1 cup light corn syrup

2 tablespoons unsalted butter, melted

1/4 cup Flying Bison Oatmeal Stout beer

Filling

- In a mixing bowl combine the eggs, brown sugar, vanilla, corn syrup, butter, and Stout. Mix until smooth and pour into chilled pie crust. Bake for 15 minutes at 375°F, then turn oven down to 350°F for approximately 30 minutes, until the center of the pie has risen.

PLATING

Allow the pie to cool thoroughly before serving. Slice and serve with caramel sauce, chocolate sauce, vanilla ice cream, or fresh berries.

99

CHALLENGE 15: BEER FROM FLYING BISON

MENU FOR CHALLENGE 15

CHALLENGING CHEF
James D. Roberts
of Park Country Club

Beer, Five Ways:
- Boutique Oyster on the Half Shell, Nitrogen-cooled Alegar Mignonette Pearls
- Crispy Chicken Wing, Oatmeal Stout Molé Negro, Toasted Sesame
- Truffled Pork Crepinette, Foie Gras, Alegar Kraut, Beer Mustard
- T-Meadow Farms Heritage Pork Taco al Pastor, Mexican Corn Tortillas
- Belgian Onion Soup, Cave-aged Gruyère

Flying Bison Oatmeal Stout-braised Kobe Beef Rib, Toasted Barley "Risotto," Caramelized Onions and Mushrooms, Beer-battered Lardon, Saaz Hops Demi-Glace, Citrus Coriander Blossoms

Double Scoop Light and Dark Beer Ice Cream Sundae, Bourbon Whipped Cream, Bourbon Caramel, Compressed Bourbon Cherries, Toasted Beer Nuts

NICKEL CITY CHEF
JJ Richert
of Torches

Beer Brat-stuffed Whole Grain Mustard Gnocchi Oatmeal Stout Fonduta, Wild Ramps, Hop Foam

The Ultimate Tailgate:
- "Hoagie" of Beer-braised Beef Short Rib with Gruyère
- "Beer Can" Squab with Bean-stuffed Zucchini Blossom
- Welsh Rarebit Mac and Cheese

Chocolate Stout Pecan Pie Oatmeal Stout Nitrogen-cooled Ice Cream, Beer Caramel

SCORES FOR CHALLENGE 15

	Challenging Chef James D. Roberts	Nickel City Chef JJ Richert	
Taste & Flavor	11	Taste & Flavor	12
Creativity	11	Creativity	12
Plating & Presentation	12	Plating & Presentation	11
Technical Execution	12	Technical Execution	12
Use of Secret Ingredient	12	Use of Secret Ingredient	9
Audience Vote	0	Audience Vote	1
Total	**58**		**57**

The Challenger:
James D. Roberts
Park Country Club
4949 Sheridan Drive, Williamsville
parkclub.org

James D. Roberts was born in New Orleans and raised in a small rural shrimping and fishing community south of the city. He was thrust into the food industry at the age of fourteen, learning and honing his trade while working in some of South Louisiana's best restaurants.

While his first love was science and chemistry, the culinary arts have proven to be his professional calling. A culinary degree from

Johnson & Wales University enhanced several years of disciplined training and apprenticeships, including an executive chef certification from the American Culinary Federation.

> While his first love was science and chemistry, the culinary arts have proven to be his professional calling.

In his current position at Park Country Club, Chef Roberts successfully leads and mentors a staff of several highly trained and driven culinary arts professionals. Tucked away in the suburbs of Buffalo, Park Country Club was founded in 1903, its building designed by architect Clifford C. Wendehack. Club members enjoy tennis courts, swimming, several dining areas, and a golf course that hosted the 1934 PGA Championship.

CHALLENGE 16

Duck Eggs

FROM PAINTED MEADOW

VS.

Nickel City Chef
Adam Goetz
Sample, Buffalo, NY

Challenging Chef
Louis Zanghi
The Delaware,
Tonawanda, NY

Painted Meadow

Franklinville, New York

Painted Meadow does a steady business with many Buffalo chefs, providing pork, lamb, goat, rabbit, duck, chicken, turkey, goose, and eggs to the city's finest restaurants.

Bonnie George has long considered herself a "farm girl," having been raised on a farm as one of nine children. As an adult, she and her husband, Donald, farmed in Bliss, New York for twenty-six years before relocating their horse ranch to Franklinville, New York in 1997. Their successful ranch leased horses to youth camps and also boarded horses for others. In 2000, the Georges decided they'd had enough of the horse trade, and instead continued solely with their side business of raising rabbits, which they sold to Asian restaurants in New York City.

Much later came duck eggs, the secret ingredient for Nickel City Chef's sixteenth challenge. It is possible to trace this unusual choice of ingredient back to April 2008. At a Buffalo First-hosted conversation among food activists, farmers, and chefs, Bonnie George was introduced to chef Bruce Wieszala (see page 28). He had just relocated from Atlanta and had a passion for local sourcing. Wieszala worked directly with Bonnie, buying rabbit and ultimately introducing her to the idea of becoming a vendor at the Elmwood-Bidwell Farmers' Market in Buffalo. Her application was accepted, and it was through her presence at the market and positive word-of-mouth that her business began to grow.

She and Donald had always raised all of their own food, including turkeys, chickens, pigs, cows, and goats. Soon, Bonnie realized that there was demand for all of those items, particularly those raised in the manner she preferred: on pasture, roaming free with a steady diet found naturally on the farm and supplemented with feed. The Georges' animals are antibiotic and hormone free, although Bonnie won't allow an injured animal to suffer. She uses the holistic and natural treatments her father taught her to treat a sick or injured animal.

Painted Meadow, as the farm has been christened, is a one-stop shop for those looking for animal proteins. Chicken, duck, turkey, goose, beef, pork, goat, lamb, and rabbit are all available. In addition, Bonnie sells chicken, duck, and goose eggs—all favorite items at the market. Her duck eggs are especially popular with chefs; a few area restaurants feature them on their regular menus. And at the final challenge of Nickel City Chef's third season, the two competing chefs made the eggs sing.

Duck eggs taste like chicken eggs, but have the added benefit of being 30 percent larger and containing more protein and minerals. They also have a slightly higher fat content, which the chefs dealt with accordingly. Duck eggs are rich in flavor and impart a creamy consistency to cooked foods— they are especially popular with pastry chefs and bakers. The demand promises to keep growing as new fans emerge, egg by egg.

The last competition of the third season, Challenge: Duck Eggs, proved to be one of the most memorable events. Not only did we have two enthusiastic chefs ready to compete using a secret ingredient with fantastic flavor and flexibility, we also had a very special judge on hand: Regina Schrambling, a New York City food critic. with a hefty coast-to-coast pedigree, agreed to come to Buffalo and sit on our panel. Called the "angriest person writing about food" by celebrity chef-turned-writer, Anthony Bourdain, Schrambling proved to be a polite guest and an honest judge, who was impressed by the dishes prepared by both chefs. She also offered some genuine criticism. Schrambling has been a regular traveler to Buffalo for years and has often extolled the city's virtues (both edible and non) in print. We were excited to show her what our Buffalo chefs could do in a Nickel City Chef competition when all creative constraints were removed.

The two chefs chose entirely different culinary directions. Challenger Louis Zanghi of The Delaware called up the ghosts of classic French cuisine, and Nickel City Chef Adam Goetz did what he does best: think outside the box.

Zanghi's first course consisted of several components, including a very rich scotch egg, a deviled egg featuring bacon and cheddar, and a Bloody Mary garnished with a wedge of pickled egg, brilliantly dyed deep purple by beet-juice brine. These simple dishes are what some might consider peasant cooking, but the presentation was attractive, and each bite was flavorful.

Goetz's first course, refined and concept-driven, couldn't have been more different: tiny bits of egg scrambled in whole butter, then served as the basis for a play on Chinese egg drop soup. A soft egg yolk, breaded, fried, and served with fresh asparagus dressed with Bearnaise sauce and a sherry vinaigrette, was also part of this course. The play between new and old, conceptual and practical carried on throughout the meal, ending with two inventive and luscious desserts.

"The whimsy and flavor profile of Goetz's dessert course—a clever dish that deceptively looked like an egg but was instead a stiff and sweet baked meringue topped with a "yolk" of lemon curd—pushed him to victory and wowed the audience and judges alike."

In the end, Goetz won by just a handful of points. The whimsy and flavor profile of his dessert course—a clever dish that deceptively looked like an egg but was instead a stiff and sweet baked coconut meringue topped with a "yolk" of lemon curd—pushed him to victory and wowed the audience and judges alike.

The duck egg challenge was a smashing end to an excellent, sold-out season, and the staff and chefs that make up Nickel City Chef felt a new sense of pride, paving the way for this book and all that promises to follow.

Nickel City Chef Adam Goetz and his sous, James Gehrke, make a strong team. Gehrke took the title in the first Nickel City Sous Chef competition, held in 2011 at the Taste of Buffalo.

CHALLENGE 16: DUCK EGGS FROM PAINTED MEADOW

Floating Islands

Servings: 4 | Total prep and cooking time: 1 hour | Preheat oven to 375°F

INGREDIENTS

1 1/2 cups Painted Meadow duck egg white
(1 cup if using chicken eggs)

1 cup powdered sugar

2 teaspoons vanilla extract

1/2 teaspoon lemon juice

4 cups whole milk

4 cups heavy cream

2 cups sugar

2 1/4 cups Painted Meadow duck egg yolk
(2 cups if using chicken eggs)

PLUS

2 cups whole milk

1 cup sugar

Nonstick pan spray

Chef's notes

The spun caramelized sugar made by Chef Zanghi works in wide open spaces or industrial kitchens. Home cooks can garnish with toasted nuts or small slices of fruit. These islands are delicious either way.

DIRECTIONS

• In a chilled bowl, beat egg whites and lemon juice until soft peaks form (with duck eggs this could take as long as 10 minutes). Slowly add 1 teaspoon of the vanilla and the powdered sugar 2 tablespoons at a time until stiff peaks form. Spray small ramekins or a mini muffin pan with nonstick spray. Line with granulated sugar. Place vessel(s) in a hot water bath in the oven. Fill with meringue mixture. Bake until the meringues double in size and are light brown. Remove from oven. Discard water bath and refrigerate meringues until ready to plate.

• In a saucepan over medium heat, combine remaining vanilla, cream, milk, and sugar. Bring to a boil, stirring constantly with a wooden spoon. Reduce to low heat. In a mixing bowl, add one cup of hot cream mixture to the yolks, mixing thoroughly. When the eggs have been tempered, add the yolk mixture to the rest of the cream. Stirring slowly and continuously, heat until the mixture reaches 180°F. Run the cream through a fine strainer and refrigerate until well chilled.

• Slowly heat the remaining milk and sugar in a sauce pan. Carefully unmold the meringues (they will have fallen by half in size) with a paring knife and drop them gently into the warm poaching liquid. Turn the meringues continuously for 1 minute or until they puff back up to their original size. Remove to a paper towel for 5 minutes.

PLATING

Pour chilled vanilla sauce into individual bowls or one large family style bowl. Add the meringues to the vanilla sauce and serve. Garnish with toasted almonds, toasted pistachios or small slices of fruit.

Nancy J. Parisi

Duck Yolk Ravioli
with Pea Purée and Lemon Vinaigrette

Servings: 4 | Total prep and cooking time: 2 hours

INGREDIENTS

1 3/4 cups all-purpose flour

12 Painted Meadow duck egg yolks

1 1/2 teaspoons extra virgin olive oil

1 tablespoon whole milk

1 egg, beaten for wash

DIRECTIONS

Ravioli

- Pour the flour onto work surface in a large mound. Using your hand, form a well in the middle. Put the oil, six of the yolks and the milk into the well and beat with a fork, slowly adding the flour from the mound into the middle, and forming a dough. When all the flour is incorporated, knead the dough for 10 minutes. Using a pasta roller on setting No. 5, roll out two pasta sheets. Cover the dough with a damp towel and set aside.

- Working on a flat surface, lay out six of the yolks evenly on a pasta sheet. Cover with the second pasta sheet. Using a sharp knife, cut the ravioli into squares, being careful not to break the egg yolks between the pasta sheets. Use the remaining beaten egg and your fingers to secure the edges of the ravioli.

2 tablespoons unsalted butter

3 cloves garlic

1 yellow onion, sliced

3 cups frozen peas, thawed

Pea Purée

- In a small sauce pan over medium heat, combine the butter, garlic, and yellow onion. Cook until tender. Add peas and cook for 1 minute. Place the pea mixture into a blender and purée until smooth. Season with salt and pepper. Hold warm to the side.

2 lemons, juiced

1 Painted Meadow duck egg yolk

1/2 cup canola oil

Salt and pepper

Lemon Vinaigrette

- Combine lemon juice and yolk in a blender. Slowly add oil while blender is still on. Season with salt and pepper to taste. Please note: *The FDA suggests that people not eat raw or uncooked egg.*

- Bring a large pot of salted water to boil over medium high heat. Add the ravioli and cook for approximately 90 seconds. The pasta should be cooked, but the yolk should remain runny. When cooked, remove and drain.

PLATING

On a plate, pool some pea purée. Top with ravioli. Drizzle with lemon vinaigrette. Slices of grape or cherry tomato make an excellent garnish.

CHALLENGING CHEF
Louis Zanghi
of The Delaware

Duck Egg Trio:
• Deviled Duck Egg with New York Cheddar and Bacon
• Scotch Egg with Whole Grain Mustard
• Bloody Mary with Pickled Duck Egg

Duck Eggs en Cocotte
Shiitake, Spinach, and Duck Confit

Floating Islands with Caramel

NICKEL CITY CHEF
Adam Goetz
of Sample

Duck Egg Quad:
• Asparagus Béarnaise with Sherry-Vinegar Reduction and Breaded Fried Egg Yolk
• Egg Drop Soup
• Crispy Braised Pork Belly with Poached Duck Egg "Drops"
• Ramos Gin Fizz

Spring Ravioli
Pea Purée, Duck Egg Tempura King Crab, Lemon Vinaigrette, Sauce Choron, Pea Shoot Tomato Salad

"Sunny Side Up Egg"
Coconut Meringue, Pineapple Curd, Cocoa Nibs, Toasted Coconut, Chocolate Biscotti

SCORES FOR CHALLENGE 16

	Challenging Chef Louis Zanghi		Nickel City Chef Adam Goetz
Taste & Flavor	11	Taste & Flavor	10
Creativity	8	Creativity	12
Plating & Presentation	10	Plating & Presentation	11
Technical Execution	12	Technical Execution	10
Use of Secret Ingredient	11	Use of Secret Ingredient	12
Audience Vote	0	Audience Vote	1
Total	**52**		**56**

The Challenger:
Louis Zanghi
The Delaware
3410 Delaware Avenue, Tonawanda

Chef Louis Zanghi received his formal education at the Culinary Institute of America in Hyde Park. He began his cooking career in Buffalo's then popular city location of Le Metro. There he was chef of both the bistro and Le Metro's artisinal bakery, recognized as Buffalo's first.

Chef Zanghi's unique combination of classical French culinary training and blue-collar, rust-belt background lent themselves well to his role as executive chef at one of the Buffalo area's new restaurants, The Delaware. This Kenmore dining establishment, offering refined, casual dining, gained instant success upon opening in December 2010.

In late 2011, Chef Zanghi and his family relocated to Tampa, Florida, where he expected to work on developing a new business model.

Chef Zanghi's unique combination of classical French culinary training and blue-collar, rust-belt background lent themselves well to his role as executive chef at one of the Buffalo area's new restaurants, The Delaware.

106

Local Food Sources

The high quality, wide variety and sheer abundance of local products available in Buffalo and Western New York make choosing to buy locally when shopping and cooking very enjoyable. The sixteen farms and food makers highlighted in the Nickel City Chef Challenges and in the chapters of this book are listed and mapped on pages 108 and 109. However, these represent a mere handful of the more than 7,500 farms and 1,000 food manufacturers located within the eight counties of Western New York. There are literally hundreds of places where these locally grown and produced foods and ingredients may be purchased, including at least fifty farmers' markets, more than a dozen CSAs (member-based farms), and hundreds of markets that source locally. This makes listing all of these resources an almost overwhelming challenge. A sampling of locations where local food can be purchased primarily in and around the city of Buffalo are listed below, but there are many more excellent locations throughout the region.

Because new resources are cropping up all the time, the online resources listed promise to provide access to the most current and reliable locations and details for Western New York's many farms, markets, wineries, CSAs, and more. Bon appétit!

Nickel City Chef's Favorite Buffalo-area Farmers' Markets

Clinton Bailey Farmers' Market
1443-1517 Clinton Street, Buffalo
Saturdays, year-round
www.clintonbaileymarket.com

Downtown Buffalo Country Market
Main Street, between Court and Church streets, Buffalo
Tuesdays and Thursdays, late May through late October
www.buffaloplace.com/downtown-country-market

Elmwood-Bidwell Farmers' Market
Bidwell Parkway and Elmwood Avenue, Buffalo
Saturday mornings, early May through mid-December
www.elmwoodmarket.org

Market at the Mill
56 East Spring Street, Williamsville
Saturdays, late May through October

Nickel City Chef's Favorite Buffalo-area Grocery Stores

Guercio & Sons
250 Grant Street, Buffalo
www.guercioandsons.com

Lexington Co-operative Market
807 Elmwood Avenue, Buffalo
www.lexington.coop

Wegmans
11 locations throughout Western New York
www.wegmans.com

Nickel City Chef's Favorite Buffalo-area Urban Farms

Community Action Organization
70 Harvard Place, Buffalo 14209
716-881-5150
www.caoec.org/html/gec.htm

Massachusetts Avenue Project (MAP)
389 Massachusetts Avenue, Buffalo
716-882-5327
www.mass-ave.org

Wilson Street Urban Farm
Wilson Street, Buffalo
716-853-7316
www.wilsonstreeturbanfarm.wordpress.com

Nickel City Chef's Favorite Buffalo-area CSAs

Native Offerings Little Valley
On-farm pick-up or drop off at three Buffalo-area locations
716-257-3006
csa@nativeofferings.com
www.nativeofferings.com

Porter Farms Elba
On-farm pick-up or drop off at 18 locations throughout Erie and Niagara counties
585-757-6823
porterfarmscsa@gmail.com
www.porterfarms.org

Promised Land Alden
On-farm pick-up or drop off at two Buffalo-area locations
585-599-3462
promisedlandcsa@gmail.com
www.promisedlandcsa.com

Online Resources for Sourcing Local Food in Western New York

Farmers' Market Federation of NY
Lists farmers' markets in New York State
www.nyfarmersmarket.com

Pick Your Own–Western New York
Lists farms that invite you to pick your own seasonal fruit and vegetables
www.pickyourown.org/nywest.htm

A Guide to Western New York CSAs
A list compiled by Buffalo Spree magazine, updated annually
Search "CSA" at www.buffalospree.com

Lake Erie Wine Country
The official website of Chautauqua County wineries
www.lakeeriewinecountry.org

Niagara Wine Trail
The official website of the Niagara County wine trail
www.niagarawinetrail.org

Local Harvest
A national website that can be searched by zip code, product, farm and market
www.localharvest.org

Eat Wild
Emphasis on grass-fed livestock, searchable by state
www.eatwild.com

Eat Local Buffalo
An offshoot of Feed Your Soul's efforts to supply resources and information
Click on the Eat Local Resources tab at www.eatlocalbuffalo.com

Nickel City Chef Secret Ingredient Sources

 Kreher's Farm (Eggs, page 11)
Clarence, NY
www.egglandsbest.com

 Spar's European Sausage (Sausage, page 17)
405 Amherst Street, Buffalo, NY 14207
716-876-6607
www.sparseuropeansausage.com

 White Cow Dairy (Yogurt, page 23)
East Otto, NY
orderfresh@aol.com
www.whitecowdairy.com

 Promised Land CSA (Potatoes, page 29)
3105 County Line Road, Corfu, NY 14036
585-599-3462
promisedlandcsa@gmail.com
www.promisedlandcsa.com

 Sorrento® (Ricotta, page 35)
Buffalo, NY
www.sorrentocheese.com

 Green Heron Growers
(Shiitake mushrooms, page 41)
2361 Wait Corners Road, Panama, NY 14767
716-753-0371
srockcastle@gmail.com
www.greenherongrowers.com

 Grape Growers' Cooperative
(Concord grape concentrate, page 47)
112 North Portage Street, Westfield, NY 14787
716-326-3161
patty@concordgrapejuice.com
www.concordgrapejuice.com

 Singer Farm Naturals (Balaton cherries, 53)
6730 Lake Road, Appleton, NY 14008
716-778-7077
info@singerfarmnaturals.com
www.singerfarmnaturals.com

 Baldwin Hill Farms (Maple, page 59)
8508 Baldwin Hill Road, Rushford, NY 14777
585-437-2106
info@baldwinhillfarms.com
www.maplelady.com

 Arrowhead Spring Vineyards (Wine, page 65)
4746 Town Line Road, Cambria, NY 14094
716-434-8030
www.arrowheadspringvineyards.com

 T-Meadow Farm (Heritage pork, page 71)
3732 Ewings Road, Lockport, NY 14094
716-434-7206
tmeadowfarm@roadrunner.com
www.heritagebreedsusa.com/TMeadow.html

 Good Grass Farm (Chicken, page 77)
2943 Open Meadows Road
Ashville, NY 14710
716-782-3322
info@goodgrassfarm.com
www.goodgrassfarm.com

 Dan Tower Farm (Apples, page 83)
1647 Youngstown Road
Youngstown, NY 14174
716-745-3370, 716-940-2645
danieltowerfarm@yahoo.com
www.dantowerfarm.com

 H2Gro (Tomatoes, page 89)
Lewiston, NY
716-754-1065
www.h2gro.net

 Flying Bison Brewing Company (Beer, page 95)
491 Ontario Street, Buffalo, NY 14207
716-873-1557
Tim@flyingbisonbrewing.com
www.flyingbisonbrewing.com

 Painted Meadow (Duck eggs, page 101)
Franklinville, NY
716-676-3401

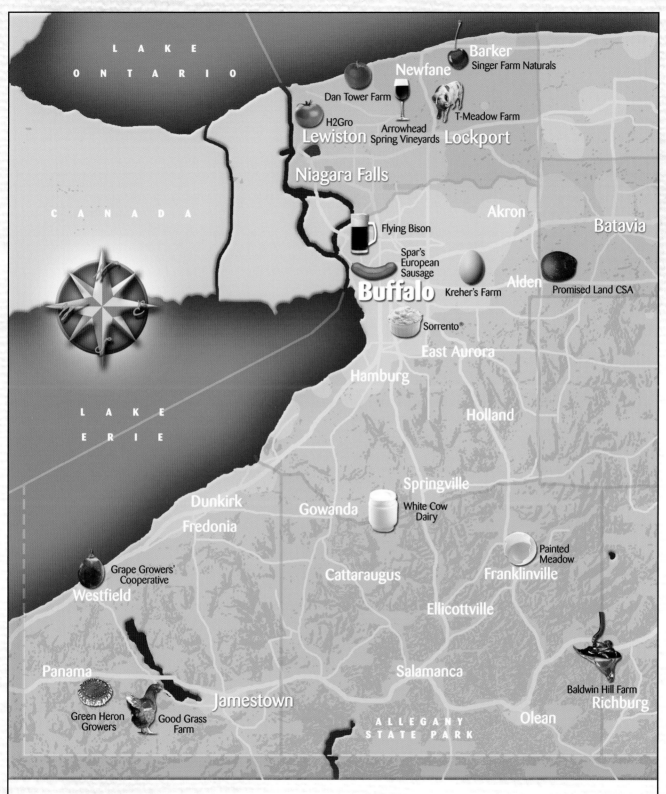

There are more than 7,500 farms in Western New York. The local ingredients used during the first sixteen Nickel City Chef challenges offer only a glimpse into the hundreds of interesting, nutritious, and flavorful agricultural items available in this region.

Index

112